MY YOUTUBE ADVENTURES

© Michael Parkinson 2024

The rights of Michael Parkinson to be identified as the author of this work have been asserted by him in accordance with sections 77 and 78 of the Copyright, Designs and Patents Act 1988.

All rights reserved. No part of this book may be reprinted or reproduced or utilised in any form or by any electronic, mechanical, or other means, now known or hereafter invented, including photocopying and recording, or in any information storage or retrieval system, without the prior written consent of the author, the author's representatives or a licence permitting copying in the UK issued by the Copyright Licensing Agency Ltd.

www.cla.co.uk

ISBN 978-1-78792-073-6

Book design, layout and production management by Into Print
www.intoprint.net, +44 (0)1604 832140

Contents

1 The Reluctant YouTuber 7

2 Colour of his Hair to Stingrays Rock and Roll 9
Including Judith Durham/Seekers Final Performance. Brahms Violin/Piano Sonata. Flamenco Stick Dance.

3 Birdsong at Eventide to Blackpool Rock Pop & Roll 13
Including Snow Waltz. Australia all out for 60, Broad 8 for 15. Psalm 23. Belle Chen, piano, extended technique

4 Children's Hymn to Disney Paris 16
Including Saara Alto sings in Leicester Square. O Holy Night. Rocky Horror Show, Time Warp. All that Jazz.

5 Joanna Forest to Nottinghamshire Police Band. 19
Including Instant piano composition. ABC Minors film song. Candyman from Willy Wonka. Dambusters March. Men of Trent

6 Two weeks on the Isle of Wight 22
Including Portsmouth to IOW Ferry. Ryde to Sandown on IOW Rail. Boogie Woogie Bugle Boy. Sunny Side of the Street. Shanklin Chine. Newclose Cricket Ground. Red Funnel at Cowes. Godshill Model Village.

7 Speed your journey to Billy Fury 25
Including Mayfair Quickstep. Pre Thursford Christmas Spectacular. Creating low maintenance Garden.

8 Yukki-Ono to Whitby. 30
Including Thames Source with water. Keyworth to Widmerpool walk. Keyworth Meadow walk.

9 Door Canopy to I've Gotta Horse 33
Including I've Gotta Horse clips. Opening credits. I'll be there to stand by you. Fire engines at Great Yarmouth. Old soft shoe. Amanda Barrie in dressing room. I like animals. Find your dreams. Tell me why. Anselmo Derby scene. Finale.

10 Billy Fury to Spread a Little Happiness 37
Including Billy Fury 81st birthday graveside tribute. Fulham riverside stand. Hammersmith bridge closed. Horses licking.

11 Scarborough Spa to Brighton Marathon 40
Including Spa programme. India and England National Anthems. Half a sixpence review.

12 Mary Poppins to Steinway Teddy Bear..43
Including Phil Kelsall. Display Screen in Peugeot 508 Car. Directions for travelling to Billy Fury grave at Westminster Mill Hill cemetery.

13 Scarborough Bus to Shepherds Hut..47
Including Swan Hotel at Staines. Staines Bridge walk to boat club. Sikh explains ceremonial dress. Staines Bridge to Laleham walk. Saturn Running Club. Cable Car over the Thames at Greenwich. Michael Parkinson driving a driverless DLR train. John Lewis Oxford Street roof garden.

14 Thames Path Walk 51
There are thirty-five titles loaded to YouTube of my Thames Path Walk.

15 Christmas Day in the Workhouse to Scottish Army in Trafalgar Square 59
Including Billy Fury by Vince Eager. BT Digital Voice Adapter. Hannah Lewis, cello.

16 Nottingham Organ Society Introduction and Year 2013........................64

17 Nottingham Organ Society year 2014 70

18 Nottingham Organ Society Year 2017 79

19 Nottingham Organ Society Year 2018 83

20 Nottingham Organ Society Year 2019 89

21 Nottingham Organ Society Year 2020 96

22 Nottingham Organ Society Year 2021 98

23 Nottingham Organ Society Year 2022 103

24 Nottingham Organ Society Year 2023 117

25 Nottingham Organ Society Year 2024 139

26 Nottingham Organ Society The first 30 years 1967/97 by Michael Carpenter ..157

27 Nottingham Organ Society The Second 30 years 1997/2027?..............162

28 St Peter's Ravenshead Gilbert & Sullivan Society............................164

29 St Peter's Ravenshead Gilbert & Sullivan Society
– The History by Karen Turner...168

30 The Eric Coates Society..175

Acknowledgements

I thank my wife, Joan for all the help she has given me in preparation of this work.

A special thank you, to Mrs Jenny Green who has edited every chapter as I have gone along.

Thank you to my YouTube Subscribers and people who have made comments on my videos.

Thank you to Anne and Mark Webb of Paragon Publishing, Into Print.

Thank you to Michael Carpenter for his history of Nottingham Organ Society.

Thank you to Karen Turner for the history of St Peter's Ravenshead Gilbert & Sullivan Society.

I acknowledge that I have used information from the Eric Coates Autobiography 'Suite in Four Movements'.

Michael Parkinson – September 2024

Foreword

Michael Parkinson

Welcome to a vast collection of stories as I guide you through my adventure. YouTube video titles are included adding sound, colour and music to the stories. You may just want to read your book in conventional style. Alternatively, you can personalise your copy by adding your own comments and information to some or all of seven hundred titles. My story became more serious when becoming the videographer at Nottingham Organ Society during 2013. My experience enabled me to adopt a similar role with the Ravenshead Gilbert and Sullivan Society and the Eric Coates Society. Comprehensive stories and histories of these organisations are included.

Other books by Michael Parkinson

From Billy Fury to YouTube	ISBN 978-1-78222-588-1
Ovaltineys to Sheredean Girls Club	ISBN 978-1-78222-675-8
Thames Path Walk	ISBN 978-1-78222-755-7
Amazing Audition	ISBN 978-1-78222-831-8
Naturism	ISBN 978-1-78222-916-2
Naturism (hardback)	ISBN 978-1-78222-924-7

Chapter 1
The Reluctant YouTuber

Back in the year 2010 a friend suggested that I should set up a YouTube Channel. My reply was 'I can't be bothered with anything like that, too difficult for me'. He countered 'With your interest in music and shows that you promote you have the perfect opportunity to load some interesting videos'. His name is John Gurnhill, a retired Maths teacher and keen long distance walker whose current YouTube channel is called r4ndym4n.

Something happened on the 9 November 2011 that persuaded me to have a go. I attended a piano recital at Steinway Hall, the showroom of Steinway Pianos. It is situated just off Oxford Street on Marylebone Lane in London's West End. The pianist was a pretty young lady from Italy, Vanessa Benelli Mosell, who was studying at the Royal College of Music, situated near the Royal Albert Hall in London. Vanessa played music composed by Domenico Scarlatti, Richard Dubugnon and Franz Liszt. As I enjoyed the performance I noticed that a lady sitting next to me was apparently making a sound recording but just before the scheduled end of the concert she sighed and pulled the connections out of her recording device. The pianist finished playing and as she was acknowledging applause I asked the lady if her battery had gone flat she said 'Yes, I'm her Mother and have travelled all the way from Italy to record her and my battery has run out'. Vanesa went off stage but returned and proceeded to play an encore, a fast piece that excited me. On impulse, I took my iPhone from my pocket and recorded the remainder of the piece. At the end, whilst Vanessa was being applauded, her Mother asked me if I could load it to YouTube. To my shame, I said 'No' because I did not know how to do it and was worried that I should not have been videoing it anyway.

We all went downstairs to a reception of wine and nibbles, provided by Steinway. Mother introduced me to Vanessa who asked if I would put her encore on YouTube and I heard myself saying 'Yes'. It was easy to ignore Mother's request but I could not refuse Vanessa. She told me that the piece was called 'Grand Galop Chromatique' written by Franz Liszt. I asked and obtained permission from the manager of Steinway to load my video to YouTube and pondered how I would do so on my train journey back to Nottingham that night. The next day I investigated how to set up a YouTube channel. An obstacle was my name because I have the same name as the well known TV personality Sir Michael Parkinson (now deceased). I decided to call my YouTube channel Michael notthatone Parkinson and loaded the video with the name

Liszt Grand Galop Chromatique, Vanessa Benelli Mosell, Piano

Date viewed:

I was pleased that the video received many views and comments so thanked my friend for his suggestion at my first opportunity. Of course, setting up the channel and loading one video was just the start of a huge learning curve. The first big thing I learned was that I could make better looking videos if I recorded in landscape instead of portrait.

I have an Apple iMac computer and found that I could edit videos using a system called Quick Time Player. I do not profess to be good when using my speaking voice to add narration to my videos but it is amazing how good editing and patience makes me sound better.

Fourteen years later I have loaded over 2400 videos to YouTube and have 2334 subscribers. People often ask 'what sort of things do you put on YouTube'. My answer is 'Anything that interests me and hopefully my viewers'. The following pages include stories and video titles that hopefully illustrate my answer.

Chapter 2

The Colour of His Hair to Stingrays

On the 5 February 2014 I videoed a concert performed by the Peacock Ensemble who are based at Trinity Laban Conservatoire of Music and Dance in Greenwich. The venue was St James's Church situated on Piccadilly, near to Piccadilly Circus, in London. The group performed for nearly an hour, the theme was 'oppression of people because of their religious or other beliefs'. I loaded ten videos to YouTube and have selected one for your interest. This is based on a poem written by A E Housman at the time of the trial and conviction of Oscar Wilde for 'gross indecency'. Because of the public attitude to homosexuality the poem was not published until after the death of Housman. The YouTube title is

Housman A E, Peacock Ensemble,The Colour of His Hair

Date viewed:

In January 2013 my wife noticed that Judith Durham and the Seekers would be performing at The Nottingham Concert Hall, The show was billed as *The Seekers 50th Anniversary – The Farewell* Tour. The show date was 25 September 2013. Although that date was months away from my birthday Joan asked me if I wanted to go as my birthday treat. I readily agreed because I had been an admirer of Judith Durham since going to see her with the Seekers at the Winter Gardens, Bournemouth in 1967. When we tried to book tickets the front stalls were fully booked and we were offered seats in what was described as Box A seats 4&5 Side View which we accepted. In May of that year we heard the devastating news that Judith had suffered a brain haemorrhage and was in intensive care at a hospital in

Melbourne. Some days later we received a letter from Nottingham Concert Hall offering the choice of our money back or waiting to find out if the show could take place at a later date. We chose the latter option in the hope that Judith would recover. In July we read a news report that stated 'Judith Durham of The Seekers says she will have to learn to read music and play the keyboard again after suffering a brain haemorrhage. But the Australian music legend is still singing. Ms Durham suffered the haemorrhage in May and has spent the past six weeks in intensive rehabilitation at a Melbourne hospital. She celebrated her 70th birthday today with members of The Seekers, including Athol Guy and Keith Potger.

Ms Durham says while her ability to read and write has been affected, her singing remains in tune. 'I'm very, very fortunate that the doctors put me to the test very early in the piece,' she said.' I think everybody around me was sort of skirting that question of can she sing still and nobody sorted of wanted to be the first to take that plunge.'

Professor John Olver of Epworth Rehabilitation says Ms Durham has been making good progress and will likely be in hospital for a few more weeks, Then we'll look at options of being out of the hospital and then eventually home and getting back to being independent at home',

Whilst we were pleased with the promising news we knew that it was doubtful that the Farewell tour would go ahead. However, some months later, we received a message from the Nottingham Concert Hall that the show had been rescheduled for 1 May 2014.

We went to the show on that date and I made sure that my iPhone battery was fully charged although I knew it was doubtful that I would be allowed to video. Our seating position was at the side of the stage with a wooden screen behind us. When Judith and the Seekers appeared on stage they received an emotional standing ovation which went on for about four minutes. This was before they had sung one note, I have never witnessed that happening before. Whilst the audience were applauding halfway through the first half Joan whispered to me that people were videoing and a quick look around the auditorium confirmed that they were.

I recommend that you search YouTube for

> Judith Durham, The Carnival is Over, Seekers final performance
> Nottingham 1 May 2014

Date viewed:

The duration of the video is 7 minutes and 32 seconds but it is worth watching to the end to see the wave and to read the 32 comments. I was in a perfect position to capture the scene as Judith was escorted around the stage on what I am sure she knew was the last time in Nottingham. I was informed by a member of staff that The Seekers had decided to allow people to video at all the venues on that tour. This even included the final show at the Royal Albert Hall in London, a truly great decision by the Seekers. Judith Durham AO (The Order of Australia) died on 5 August 2022 and a State Memorial Service to honour and celebrate her life was held on 6 September 2022 at Hamer Hall.

On 29th May 2014, I videoed a Park Lane Group, Young Artists Scheme, Lunchtime Concert. The venue was St James's Church, Piccadilly, London. The performers were Soh-Yon Kim, violin accompanied by Jennifer Lee, piano. They played music composed by Maurice Ravel and Johannes Brahms. I believe that watching and listening to music is an art form and have selected one of the pieces that I loaded to YouTube from that concert as an illustration of what I mean. The title is

Brahms Violin/Piano Sonata 3 Soh-Yon Kim 2nd movement

Date viewed:

Joan and I went on holiday to the Riu Bel Playa Hotel at Torremolinos in Spain in May 2014 and I was given permission to video the Flamenco Cabaret. We enjoyed many holidays at that Hotel which was right next to the beach. There was a lovely promenade that we could take a steady walk and refresh ourselves at one of the many beach bars along the way. The YouTube title of the famous stick dance is

Flamenco, Isobel Marques, Stick Dance at Riu Bel Playa Hotel Spain

Date viewed:

I am sure it will remind you of your holidays abroad.

In August 2014 we were staying at the Red Lea Hotel in Scarborough and noticed an influx of younger people at breakfast. Joan and I spoke to some of them and found out that they were Rock n Roll musicians and their families. My interest was kindled when the told me that they were going to perform at the Scarborough Spa Suncourt on that Sunday afternoon. I asked if I could video them with the possibility of loading to YouTube and the answer was an enthusiastic, Yes. The Scarborough Orchestra play at that venue on Sunday mornings so we enjoyed their concert as usual.

Joan and I went back to the Suncourt in the early afternoon, allowing time for me to set up my tripod. I use a device that I have made myself to hold my iPhone on the tripod so that I can pan and tilt. The young musicians call themselves the Stingrays and we discovered that they are from Essex. They played guitars and were accompanied by a drummer, and played a large variety of songs. It is always difficult to decide what to load to YouTube so I loaded everything that I had recorded because the beauty of that media is that viewers can decide what to watch. The names of some of the other pieces I loaded were, Matchbox, Peggy Sue, Oh Boy and many others. A lovely feature about their performance was the number of people who got up and danced. I have selected just one title for inclusion in this book, the YouTube title is

Stingrays, Roll Over Beethoven at Scarborough

Date viewed:

Join in and dance if you wish.

Chapter 3

Birdsong at Eventide to Blackpool

I am a member of the Eric Coates Society and videoed a concert promoted by them in October 2014. It took place at the Central Methodist Church at Hucknall which is situated close to where Eric was born on 27 August 1886. The Hucknall Torkard Ensemble performed a lovely song with music written by Eric Coates the YouTube title is

    Birdsong at Eventide, Hucknall Torkard Ensemble October 2014

Date viewed:

In December 2014 I videoed a concert performed by the Rose Singers at the Mechanics Institute in Nottingham. Danielle Hall who was a presenter on Notts TV is the musical Director of the choir, she can be seen carefully coaxing them at 1 minute 5 seconds into the video. The YouTube title is

    Snow Waltz, (Schneewalzer), Rose Singers, Nottingham Dec 2014

Date viewed:

Joan and I are members of Nottinghamshire County Cricket Club and in August 2015 attended the Test Match between England and Australia at Trent Bridge. England won the toss and decided to bowl first. It in was dull and cloudy, conditions that usually give some help to fast bowlers. The match was scheduled to last for five days so I expected Australia to bat for over a day and score more than 300 runs. I had taken my iPhone with me to video the teams entering the field and was delighted that England took two wickets in the first over. This prompted me to video the unusual score of ten runs for two wickets. Wickets fell at regular intervals and Australia were all out for sixty runs before lunch. Stuart Broad took 8 wickets bowling from the Pavilion end which has now been renamed 'The Stuart Broad End'. The video title is

Cricket England skittle Australia for 60, Broad 8 for15, August 2015

Date viewed:

On the 1 April 2012 I promoted a show entitled 'Michael Parkinson's Billy Fury Show' at the Floral Pavilion, New Brighton. The theatre is on the sea front of the Mersey Estuary and looks out towards Liverpool Docks where young Ronald Wycherley had worked on a tugboat before finding fame and fortune as Billy Fury. A bronze statue of the 1960s Rock 'n' Roll star stands on the dockside near the Museum Of Liverpool. The show featured dancers from The Anamal Dance Company from Hoylake, Claire Knight Dance School from the Wirral, Nicky Figgins Centre Stage Academy from Blackpool and Wallasey School of Ballet from Liscard. I originally had put the show on in Nottingham, Mansfield and Lytham St Annes but the Floral Pavilion show was the biggest and best featuring three narrators and one hundred and twenty-eight dancers. Scene twelve featured the announcement of the death of Billy Fury and I had decided to include the dancers who were taking part in that scene to sing the Psalm 23. This had been sung at the funeral service at St John's Wood Church in North London. I had written the script for my show and accept that directing a group of dancers to sing a Psalm as part of a dance show was probably the zaniest thing I have ever done. The video captures those young ballet dancers doing something out of their comfort zone. I am proud of what they achieved and included all the names in the description. The YouTube title is

Psalm 23, Tune Crimond, Wallasey School of Ballet

Date viewed:

On 29 June 2016 I was given permission to video a Park Lane Group Young Artists Series concert at St James's Church, Piccadilly, London. The performer was pianist Belle Chen who announced 'The last piece that I am going to play is called Black Earth, it is written by Turkish pianist/composer Fazil Say. What you would hear in the beginning is an imitation of a particular folk instrument, very special to Turkey so that is the sound that is going to evoke'. She then sat at the piano and played in a conventional manner for a few seconds before leaning forward and placing her left hand inside the piano. It was obvious that she was dampening some of the strings to create the sounds that she had described. It was the most amazing performance that I have ever witnessed and I have discovered that the procedure is called Extended Technique. I loaded the video to YouTube to an immediate reaction including a 'share' from maestro Fazil Say himself. As I write a decade later the video has received 18,819 views, 81 comments and 490 likes. The YouTube video title is

Fazil Say-Black Earth, Belle Chen Piano, extended technique

Date viewed:

In October 2016 Joan and I enjoyed a few days in Blackpool and went to the Kings and Queens of Rock and Pop show at the Central Pier Theatre. When we went in I asked permission to video with a view to loading to YouTube. I was introduced to the manager, 'Big Dave' who gave permission and agreed with my request to sit at the front for a good viewing position. I videoed all of the first half and edited it down to about 15 minutes. In June 2024 the video has received over 10.000 views with a mixture of good and bad comments. The YouTube title is

Kings & Queens of Rock Pop & Roll, Act 1 Blackpool

Date viewed:

Chapter 4

Children's Hymn to Disney Paris

On 1 October 2016, I videoed the Eighth Annual Eric Coates Concert at the Central Methodist Church at Hucknall near Nottingham. The Southwell Minster Girl's Choir were the main performers and they sang Children's Hymn (Gods Great Love Abiding). Eric had been asked to write something for a Sunday School Anniversary concert of the Baptist Church in Watnall Road which took place on 25 May 1947. On submitting his work Eric wrote 'I have written this (Children's Hymn) specially for children; it is quite short and somewhat on the lighthearted side. – I don't think children want to sing anything too serious. The words are my own and are meant to be a picture of my early days in Hucknall when I used to wander about the dusty lanes on my bicycle before motor cars used to come along and spoil the peace of the countryside. Eric was born on 27 August 1886 so his cycling would have been during the late 1890s and included the roads around Southwell Minster. It is a great tribute to his memory that this song was sung by the Southwell Minster Girls Choir in an Eric Coates Society concert around 120 years after young Eric had cycled in the area. I was proud to video the performance but the next day received the devastating news that one of the singers, who was severely facially disfigured, had refused to allow vision to be included on YouTube. I used the sound and added on screen words to my YouTube loading. The YouTube title is

Children's Hymn, Words and Music by Eric Coates

Date viewed:

As I walked through Leicester Square on 7 December 2016 I noticed a film crew who were filming a lady wearing a long white coat, I approached the crew and asked what they were doing, they told me that they were interviewing an X factor contestant. I asked if I could video and was told, Yes, and you can ask her some questions if you like. I walked up close and discovered that her name was Saara Aalto. I was at a distinct disadvantage because I did not watch X Factor and knew nothing about her but stumbled through a few questions. A man who appeared to be in charge said 'Just one more question and then we'll cut'. Saara walked into the offices of Global Radio and emerged a few minutes later. On impulse I asked if she could sing me a few notes and she immediately obliged with a few lines of 'Over the Rainbow'. It is on YouTube, title

> Saara Aalto, Dancing on Ice, X Factor Sings in Leicester Square for Michael Parkinson

Date viewed:

In December 2016 Joan and I travelled to London to attend the Phab Christmas Concert at St James's Church, Piccadilly. Phab is an organisation that 'Inspires and supports disabled and non-disabled children, young people and adults to make more of life together'. The concert was performed by The London Orpheus Choir and I loved their rendition of 'Oh Holy Night' with a young soloist and organist Ian Le Grice. The Musical Director was Richard Jenkinson. I am not allowed to give the name of the soloist because a few weeks after I had loaded the video to YouTube she sent me a message asking me to remove her name because there were a couple of imperfections in her performance. Fortunately, she did not ask me to delete the video but this does illustrate the difficulties that I encounter. On the credit side two lovely comments were made on the video, they are. 1 One of the very best versions of Oh Holy Night on YouTube, brings home the true meaning of Christmas and Thanks to Michael Parkinson for sharing this. 2 The soloists voice is beautifully suited to the music and it is one of the most moving performances of this piece which I have ever heard. Perhaps you would like to witness the performance and form your own opinion. The Youtube title is

> O Holy Night, London Orpheus Choir, Phab Christmas Concert 2016

Date viewed:

In February 2017 I was given permission to video a concert at the Festival Hall, Kirkby in Ashfield, Nottinghamshire. The band were the Kirkby Colliery Welfare Band, under MD Neville Buxton. They played Time Warp from the Rocky Horror Show, something that I had not heard a Brass Band perform before. I thought it was an excellent arrangement. The YouTube title is

Rocky Horror Show, Time Warp, Kirkby Colliery Band, Notts 2017

Date viewed:

Another piece the band performed was from the show called Chicago so I just have to include another YouTube title for you to enjoy

All That Jazz, Chicago, Kirkby Colliery Band, Notts

Date viewed:

In July 2017 Joan and I plus other family members went to Disneyland Paris for a week. We travelled by train from Nottingham and thoroughly enjoyed ourselves but my favourite ride was called It's a small world which involved sitting in a boat which took us on a ride with lovely displays on both sides. I loved the simple tune and song 'Its a small world'. We went on it four times during the five days that we were there. Perhaps you have seen it and done it but you can enjoy it by looking at this YouTube title.

Disneyland Paris, It's a small world, Michael Parkinson's favourite

Date viewed:

CHAPTER 5

JOANNA FOREST TO NOTTINGHAMSHIRE POLICE BAND

In September 2017 Joan and I were in Brighton and booked into the Little Theatre for a concert by Joanna Forest. She was billed as a 'crossover singer' but we had no idea what to expect. We arrived at the theatre early and I asked if I could video and possibly load to YouTube. After a delay whilst they consulted the artist I was given permission and told where I could sit so that I was not interfering with other audience members. As Joanna sang I videoed and noticed that she appeared to be totally flat chested. She spoke to the audience between songs and I discovered the terrible reason, She announced that she had contacted breast cancer at the age of 21 and had undergone a double mastectomy operation including chemotherapy and radiotherapy treatment. I was impressed that she had carried on with her career and was performing a whole solo concert. At the end of the show Joanna spoke to many members of the audience including Joan whilst I spoke with her husband James who told me his side of the story. I have loaded a few songs that Joanna sang to YouTube, here is the title of one of them

Time To Say Goodbye, Joanna Forest, Little Theatre, Brighton

Date viewed:

In February 2018 I asked, and was granted permission, to load to YouTube an unusual skill that pianist Mitra Alice Tham possessed. She had demonstrated it in a concert that I had promoted in April 2001 at the Djanogly Recital Hall situated in the grounds of Nottingham University. Mitra had not given permission to show her special skill in a YouTube loading at that time but relented, many years later, when I explained that Mrs Iris Broughton who had provided the theme was eager to see it. Back in January 1998 Mitra had been a student at the Purcell School for musically gifted children and was selected to perform her unusual gift for His Royal Highness, The Prince of Wales, (now HRH King Charles III) during his official visit to the school. That instant composition was aired on radio in the evening and the story was featured in the London newspapers. Her performance was described as 'brilliant and excellent' by Prince Charles. My suggested video shows Mitra Alice Tham in my April 2001 concert, she struggled to get a volunteer for some time before Iris Broughton saved the day. (Iris is a retired school pianist) and can be seen providing the theme that Mitra was pleading for. You, the reader, can decide what you think by looking at my YouTube title

Piano instant composition for Iris by Mitra Alice Tham

Date viewed:

This is a memory from my childhood, back in the late 1940s. We kids used to flock to the ABC Metropole Cinema in Sherwood Nottingham on Saturday mornings to see film shows specially selected for young children (ABC was a national chain so there could have been one where you lived). Kids that had a birthday in the previous week were invited to stand on stage whilst the ABC song was sung. About 70years later I heard an Organist playing that tune. Here are the words that we sang:-

We are the girls and boys well known as,
Minors of the ABC
And every Saturday all line up
To see the films we like and shout aloud with glee
We like to laugh and have a sing song
Just a happy crowd are we (we elongated)
We are all pals together
We're minors of the ABC

The organist that I videoed playing the tune many years later was Claire Greig so I invite readers to listen to the tune and read (or even sing) those words that provide a memory from my happy days of youth. YouTube title is

> Childhood memories, ABC Minors Saturday morning Cinema Club song

Date viewed:

In June 2018 I videoed the Nottingham Community Youth Choir at the Dales Centre Sneinton, near Nottingham. The Musical Director encouraged members of the choir to show, with their facial expressions, that they enjoyed performing and they certainly achieved that. The concert was in aid of the Samaritans charity. The YouTube link is

> Candyman (Willy Wonka), Nottingham Community Youth Choir, singing for Samaritans

Date viewed:

In October 2018 I videoed the Annual Concert organised by the Eric Coates Society at the Central Methodist Church in Hucknall. The Nottinghamshire Police Band performed the Dambusters March and another piece written by Eric Coates which he called 'Men of Trent'. This was adopted as the Regimental March of the Police Band and they performed it to perfection. The two YouTube titles are:-

> Dambusters March, Eric Coates, Nottinghamshire Police Band

Date viewed:

> Men of Trent, Eric Coates, Nottinghamshire Police Band

Date viewed:

Chapter 6

Two weeks on the Isle of Wight

On 8 May 2019 Joan and I travelled to the Isle of Wight at the start of a fortnights holiday. We are members of Nottinghamshire County Cricket Club and history was made because, from May 20th to 23rd a four day County Championship match was played at Newclose Cricket Club between Hampshire and Nottinghamshire. It was the first time that County Cricket had been played on the Island. We had decided to combine cricket and a holiday where Joan had never been before. We went by train to Portsmouth and a ferry across to Ryde. The YouTube title of that short sea crossing is

>   Portsmouth to Isle of Wight on Wightlink Catamaran Ferry 15 May 2019

Date viewed:

On arrival at Ryde we went on the Island Line train to Sandown and found that the trains used were old London Underground carriages that were ideal for going under the many low bridges on the island. The YouTube video title is

>   Isle of Wight Railway, Ryde to Sandown with Michael Parkinson

Date viewed:

When we arrived at Sandown Station we met a young man who was selling books and his collection of CDs at the station. He told us that he and his friends would be performing on the Island Line Train on 18 May as part of a 'Music on the Move programme' He invited Joan and me to go along and to my surprise we were invited onto the train free of charge because they were aware that I would be videoing and loading to YouTube. They were happy to gain the publicity, two singers who called themselves 'The Bunker Girls' performed on the Island Train as it rattled along. I loaded one of their songs to YouTube with this title

> Boogie Woogie Bugle Boy, The Bunker Girls, Live on Island Line Train IOW

Date viewed:

After we had been riding on the train and enjoying the entertainment for a couple of hours we got off at Ryde harbour and saw the young man who we had met at Sandown. I learned that his name is Mark Thomas. He was playing Ukulele and his friend J.C Grimshaw was on Guitar. We enjoyed watching them perform and speaking with them for a while. The You Tube title is

> On the Sunny Side of the Street, Ukulele and Guitar, IOW, Music on the Move

Date viewed:

One day we enjoyed a pleasant walk along the coast to Shanklin and visited the Chine, a fascinating experience with running water and lovely views. I discovered the story about the Pluto Pipeline. A very helpful guide explained background information to me as we came away but did not want to be in vision so I had to include sound only on my YouTube video

> Shanklin Chine, Isle of Wight, including Pluto pipeline

Date viewed:

We attended all four days of the cricket match and sat with two Hampshire members who we had met at Trent Bridge a few years earlier. We went for meals together at Newport in the evenings after play had finished for the day. Hampshire won the game by a large margin of 244 runs but that was the only blight on a thoroughly enjoyable match played in a lovely rural setting. My YouTube title about the ground is.

> Newclose Cricket Ground, Isle of Wight, Hugh Griffiths, How it happened

Date viewed:

On one occasion we went along to Cowes on the service buses and Joan took over videoing duties because she was impressed by how close we were to the various craft on the water. This is the YouTube video that Joan created

> Red Funnel at Cowes, Isle of Wight, Videoed by Joan Parkinson

Date viewed:

We stayed at the Sandringham Hotel in Sandown and used the excellent bus service, combined with our Senior Bus Passes throughout the fortnight, to explore the whole of the island. No visit to the Isle of Wight is complete without going to the model village at Godshill and we pulled this in on a lovely sunny day.

The model village appears to be constructed in a large ravine so that visitors walk around the top whilst looking down over lakes, sports grounds, and many other themes. I liked the addition of music at the bandstand, village hall dancing and the church which added audio pleasure to the visual delights. It is an amazing experience but the best way to see and hear what it is like is to view my YouTube video

> Godshill Model Village, Isle of Wight. Videoed by Michael Parkinson

Date viewed:

At the end of the holiday we returned to Keyworth near Nottingham by again using the Island Line train, the WightLink Fast Cat Ferry and trains from Portsmouth to Waterloo and St Pancras to East Midlands Parkway station. We loved that holiday and writing about it brings back many happy memories.

Chapter 7

Speed your journey to Billy Fury

In August 2019 Joan and I were on holiday in Scarborough. A fellow guest at the Red Lea Hotel, who we see at the Scarborough Spa Orchestra Concerts, told us that she was going to a Male Voice Choir concert at the Queen Street Methodist Church that night. Joan and I decided to go and offered to share a taxi with the Lady who had told us about it. To our surprise she said that she would take us in her car provided we did not mind that she was collecting her friend on the way. When we arrived at the Church I asked and was given permission to video and to load to YouTube. The large audience really enjoyed the performance. My favourite was 'The Chorus of the Hebrew Slaves' from Giuseppe Verdi's Opera Nabuco. The Musical Director was Thom Meredith with piano accompaniment by Keith Follow. The YouTube title is

Speed Your Journey, Colne Valley Male Voice Choir at Scarborough

Date viewed:

The following October Joan and I went to Blackpool for a few days so made our annual visit to the Tower Ballroom where we enjoyed watching the dancing and doing a bit ourselves. We sat amongst a group of people who told us they were going to the Euston Hotel at Fleetwood for an afternoon dance on the following Thursday. They convinced me that I would be welcome to video so I went along and made sure the Manager of the Hotel had no objection to me videoing. The people I had met in the Tower made me very welcome and introduced me to keyboard player Ian Midgley who gave me permission to video and suggested I position myself next to him so that I would get a good view of the dancers. I was aware I could not video the dancers without their permission so, by arrangement with Ian I, made a little speech where I explained my intention to video but only if they all agreed. There were no objections so I was all set to go. Here is the list of dances that I videoed and loaded to YouTube:-

Mayfair Quickstep

Date viewed:

Melody Foxtrot

Date viewed:

Ballroom Quickstep

Date viewed:

Square Tango

Date viewed:

White City Waltz

Date viewed:

Sindy Swing

Date viewed:

Tayside Tango

Date viewed:

Broadway Quickstep

Date viewed:

Glenroy Foxtrot

Date viewed:

Sally Ann Cha Cha

Date viewed:

Argentine Stroll

Date viewed:

Saunter Sharaz

Date viewed:

Last Waltz

Date viewed:

The whole afternoon was really enjoyable, everyone was friendly, Ian even invited me to introduce a couple of dances. If you like dancing you could experience the Tea Dance at the Euston Hotel at Fleetwood on a Thursday afternoon. It is nice to realise this is just one of many similar events that happen.

All 13 dances are loaded to YouTube but I have just chosen my favourite for the YouTube title, it is

Mayfair Quickstep, Ian Midgley, Dancers Euston Hotel Fleetwood near Blackpool

Date viewed:

In November 2019 Joan and I attended the Thursford Christmas Spectacular again, we first went in year 2010 and have been going every year since. I have loaded many videos about the event to YouTube but recommend that you look at a video which was made in 2016 by one of the dancers involved in the show. It is full of fun and zany clips. The creator is Natalie Davies who includes these words in the information about her video. *'As our three months living and performing in Norfolk is coming to an end, the Thursford dancers would like to wish you all a very merry Christmas! I do not own the copyright to this music'.*

The YouTube title is

Thursford Christmas Spectacular 2016 Dancers Merry Christmas

Date viewed:

If you watch it to the end you will see some funny out takes as well. People are not allowed to video whilst the show is in progress but can video inside before and at the end of the show. This is my YouTube video before the show started:-

Thursford before the Christmas Spectacular 2019

Date viewed:

My Granddaughter, Claire, bought a house in 2017. The garden had been neglected for many years and was in a terrible state. On 27 December 2018, my wife, Joan and I started to reclaim the garden. Our self imposed mandate was to make it easy for Claire to look after it as she is a career lady with little time to spare. She adamantly did not want a lawn so we made as much patio area and paths as possible. We finished the project on 9 January 2020 when I was 80 years of age and Joan 72. This is just another example of what grandparents do for their family. There was an old shed in the garden that Claire did not want so

I took it down and used the ends and sides to form a fence at the bottom of the garden. This is the title of a YouTube video that I loaded in January 2020 –

Garden made for easy care by Joan and Michael

Date viewed:

I have to confess I was not impressed when Claire told me she planned to paint the fence purple but she did it to perfection. It can be seen in a video that I loaded to YouTube four years later when the plants and vegetables were growing. The YouTube title is –

Garden made for easy care by Joan and Michael 4 years later, June 2024

Date viewed:

I visited the grave of Billy Fury at Westminster cemetery, Mill Hill in North London on 28th of January 2020. It is a testament to his continued popularity that the grave is a blaze of floral tributes with two lovely poems from Myra Love. I took two bunches of roses which had been bought by my wife, Joan, an ardent Billy Fury fan. Here is the title of the YouTube video tribute.

Billy Fury, floral and poetic graveside tributes – 28 January 2020

Date viewed:

Chapter 8
Yukki-Onna to Whitby

Yuki-Onna, Snow Woman, is an infamous character of Japanese Folklore. I became aware of it whilst attending a concert at Morley College, London, on 28 February 2020. Japanese pianist Haruko Seki combines Japanese and English literary Culture in her role of Head of Piano Studies at the College. This story from a book written by Yakumo Koizumi has been adapted by Mathew Wright into modern English. It is read by Susan Woods. Videoed and loaded to YouTube by Michael Parkinson

Yuki-Onna, Japanese Ghost Story, read by Susan Woods

Date viewed:

When I walked to the source of the River Thames in August 2016 I was disappointed that there was no water there so it became my ambition to see water emerging from the heap of stones that marked the source. After heavy rainfall in the winter of 2020 I checked that there was water at the stones and on 11 March 2020 I travelled from my home in Keyworth, Nottingham by train to St Pancras, London and on to Paddington where I boarded a train bound for Kemble in Gloucestershire. My plan was to video water at the source of the Thames and to walk down the meadow to Kemble Bridge. On arrival at Kemble Station there were two small taxis and a large ten seater taxi. The two small taxis were occupied by people before me in the queue so that meant that I had to clamber into the large one. I asked the driver to drop me at the little lay by about half a mile past the Thames Head Inn on the A433 Road which runs from Tetbury to Cirencester so I was close to the source of the River Thames. The driver refused and said he could only drop me in the car park of the Thames Head Inn. This meant I had to walk for half a mile along the side of the busy Road before arriving at the path leading to the source. It was a cold, windy, day with a clear blue sky that was good for vision but not for sound, sometimes hampered by noise of wind in the camera. I really enjoyed seeing water covering the heap of stones at the source before forming a small stream as it meandered down the meadow. There were many little tributaries on both sides before it merged with a fast flowing wide stream just before flowing under Kemble Bridge. I marvelled that this was to become the mighty River Thames and that it was 184 miles to the Thames Barrier at Greenwich. I really enjoyed walking and sloshing my way down the meadow and videoed the first culvert and small bridges. There were frequent pauses to take video which included my muddy Wellingtons. When I eventually arrived at Kemble Station I had just missed a train and had to wait for nearly an hour for the next one. This was overcrowded with people coming back from Cheltenham Races. I could not find a seat so had to stand until the train stopped at Swindon where I was pleased to sit in comfort by a window. I travelled home after a really enjoyable day and the following day edited the video clips that I had taken and loaded the video to YouTube with the title

Thames Source, With Water to Kemble Bridge, March 2020 by Michael Parkinson

Date viewed:

I was eighty years old at that time and five days after the journey my wife and I fell ill with COVID-19. Many experts said that Cheltenham Races should have been cancelled but hindsight is a wonderful thing. As you may gather from reading this, I did not die but decided to write my Thames Path Walk book whilst I was self isolating. The book ISBN978-1-78222-755-7 can be bought on eBay. The YouTube Title is

Thames Source, With Water to Kemble Bridge, March 2020 by Michael Parkinson

Date viewed:

In March 2020 the dreaded Covid-19 struck and the lifestyle of many people changed. When I was fit enough, I found local walks to enjoy, my favourite was along bridleways and narrow paths from Keyworth to Widmerpool in Nottinghamshire. My commentary included a mistake because I encountered a herd of what I called llamas but found out later that they were alpacas. I included

Widmerpool churchyard and continued along Old Hall Drive to include figures of a Dutch couple carved from the trunk of a huge Canadian Redwood Tree. An unusual feature of the carving is that the couple are holding an old fashioned spade and fork but the lady is also holding a mobile phone. I received a message about this video that brought immense pleasure to me, it read. *'A friend of Michael Parkinson sent this video link to a lady on her 91st birthday on 1st June 2020. This is what the birthday lady replied:-You made a 91 year old lady very happy today. Good afternoon, What a delightful surprise to receive your birthday greeting, together with a walk through the countryside. It was so lovely, and to hear the birds singing was an added treat. Thank you so very much for your kind thought, the way Michael guided us through the whole walk was certainly the next best thing to be actually on it with him, he was quite the shadowy figure.'* The YouTube title is

Keyworth to Widmerpool, Walk in South Notts with Michael Parkinson

Another local walk turned out to be a bit like 'Down Your Way' because I met many people who I talked with along the way. They ranged from people that I knew to four youths who were complete strangers but very sociable. If I had, stage managed it, I could not have done better. My video lasts for eighteen minutes, and if you watch it to the end your will see the sights of Keyworth meadow accompanied by the sound of birds whistling and see the young men. The YouTube title is

Keyworth Meadow Nature Reserve Walk, with Michael Parkinson

Date viewed:

In August 2020 Joan and I enjoyed a bus ride from Scarborough to Whitby on a hot Summer's day. I videoed Harry Hayley who was entertaining crowds of people who were walking along the Swing Bridge. The bridge opens regularly to allow boats to pass in and out of the inland part of the Harbour. The YouTube title is:-

Can You Feel the Love Tonight, Holiday crowds at Whitby, Yorkshire August 2020

Date viewed:

CHAPTER 9

DOOR CANOPY TO I'VE GOTTA HORSE

In September 2020 I purchased a Door Canopy Awning Shelter, Patio Roof Type size 120 cm by 75 cm, from eBay to fix on the outside wall over our back door. I started to fix it myself but encountered a problem. The fixings supplied were called setscrews and some of these lined up with the frogs in the bricks so I could not get a secure fixing. I found that I could use screw bolts, with suitable plastic plugs, instead. These can be tightened up with a spanner making a more secure fixing. Joan and I videoed whilst we did the job and I edited a video describing the procedure and loaded it to YouTube. My idea was to help other people who may have encountered the same problem as me. At the time of writing (July 2024) the video has achieved 15,503 views and some complimentary comments. There were a few questions that I answered to the best of my ability. I have often found something on YouTube that has solved a problem for me so I was pleased to load something to help others. The YouTube title is

Door canopy, eBay, installing with different bolts

Date viewed:

Whilst preparing for one of my Billy Fury Dance Shows at the Mansfield Palace Theatre in October 2011 I was contacted by Mr Roy Newton who told me that his wife, Christine had a personal story about her family meeting Billy Fury and the cast of his film 'I've Gotta Horse'. Christine contacted me and sent me her story which I include here exactly as she wrote it to me:-

I was staying in a caravan, on holiday, at a site at Caister-on-Sea, in Norfolk

with my parents, Dorothy and Thomas Peck.

On Monday 24th September 1964 we went to a horse-riding stables (after a lot of pestering on my part). Unfortunately, there was no riding that day because the stables had been loaned to a film crew who were filming 'I've Gotta Horse' featuring Billy Fury, The Bachelors and Leslie Dwyer.

We were allowed to stay and watch the filming, and have our pictures taken with the cast, as they wanted to keep it a secret and didn't want us going off and telling other people.

Also during the holiday (I think the same day as the filming) we went to see the Billy Fury Show at a theatre in Great Yarmouth (I think it was the Britannia Theatre). We went into Great Yarmouth early so we could have some tea first and, when we got there, fire engines were just roaring up to the Theatre. At first we thought the Theatre was on fire and the show would be cancelled but then we saw they were filming again.

My married name is Mrs Christine Newton but I was Christine Peck then and it was six weeks before my fifteenth birthday.

I thanked Christine for her story, incorporated it into the script, and presented her with a DVD copy when we met her after the show. This is my favourite Billy Fury film and I have loaded some extracts to YouTube.

The first is the opening credits and scene one. The film company allowed Billy to include some of his own animals in the picture and some outdoor location filming was shot in and around Great Yarmouth. The You Tube title is

> I've Gotta Horse, Billy Fury Film, Opening credits

Date viewed:

The second clip features Billy Fury performing a song with his backing group 'The Gamblers' in rehearsal for the drink addicted show director. The YouTube title is

> Billy Fury I'll be there to stand by you, from film 'I've Gotta Horse'

Date viewed:

The next sequence shows fire engines speeding through the streets of Great Yarmouth for what turned out to be a false alarm. This is what Christine describes in her story. The YouTube title is

> Billy Fury – Great Yarmouth Fire Engines 1965 in film 'I've Gotta Horse'

Date viewed:

Billy Fury used a cane and straw hat as he danced in a choreographed routine with a group of dancers for, what I believe, would be the first time in his career. The YouTube title is

> Billy Fury, Old Soft Shoe, Song and Dance from 'I've Gotta Horse'

Date viewed:

Amanda Barrie played the character of Jo in the film and was keen on Billy Fury. She readily agreed when Billy invited her to 'Come in the dressing room with me while no one is looking' but the scene that greeted her was not the romantic setting she had anticipated. The YouTube title is

> Billy Fury and Amanda Barrie, Horseplay in the dressing room

Date viewed:

The Bachelors were a group of singers from Dublin, Ireland, who enjoyed many top hits in the 1960s and were introduced to Christine and her family when they visited the stables. These are seen before the singers rode along the sand dunes. The YouTube title is

> When your far, away, The Bachelors-Billy Fury Film 'I've Gotta Horse'

Date viewed:

People say, 'Never work with animals or children' but Billy Fury did both in this song. The YouTube title is

> I like Animals Billy Fury and children from film 'Ive Gotta Horse'

Date viewed:

Amanda Barrie and Billy Fury appeared to be linked romantically in this excerpt. The YouTube link is

    Find your dreams, Billy Fury and Amanda Barrie, I've Gotta Horse

Date viewed:

There was a sad element where Billy was told that his pet horse, Armitage, had died prompting a solo song with scenes of the beach in Yarmouth. The YouTube title is

    Billy Fury, Tell me why, From I've Gotta Horse

Date viewed:

I understand that some of this scene was filmed at Yarmouth Races and other clips at Epsom Racecourse where a horse named Anselmo, owned by Billy Fury, finished fourth in the 1964 Derby. The writers of I've Gotta Horse used their artistic licence and innuendo into the story. My wife Joan was a Billy Fury fan, when she was a young teenager and she wanted to put a small bet on Anselmo in the 1964 Derby but was too young to go into a Betting Shop. She asked her Mother to put the bet on for her which was done as an 'each way bet'. Joan can remember people explaining what that meant but can't remember how much the bet was or how much she won. As I write, in July 2024, that was sixty years ago, but it adds interest to the story of the film. The YouTube title is

    I've Gotta Horse, Billy Fury, Armitage/Anselmo Derby Race Clip

Date viewed:

After the excitement of Billy Fury's Horse achieving success at Epsom the team had to get back to Great Yarmouth for the evening performance of the Billy Fury Show. The YouTube title of the Finale is

    Billy Fury I've Gotta Horse, Final Scene

Date viewed:

Chapter 10

Billy Fury Tribute to Spread a Little Happiness

Ronald Wycherley who achieved fame as Britain's first Rock n Roll recording star was born on the 17 April 1940, he would have been 81 in 2021. Because of Covid travel restrictions I was advised not to travel to the grave in Mill Hill Cemetery in North London on 17 April 2021. I have compiled this tribute from a visit that Joan and I did in 2017, Michael Parkinson. The YouTube title is

Billy Fury 81st Birthday Tribute 17 April 2021

Date viewed:

On 19 May 2021 I walked along the Thames Path on the South side of the River starting at Putney Bridge and soon noticed that construction of the Fulham Football Club stand was progressing well. I understand the original plan was to cantilever the construction partially over the River but this met with widespread local opposition. Work started in 2019 and I understand the revised plan will include a roof top swimming pool. I spoke to a local man who told me that when completed walkers will be allowed to walk along the Thames Path, passing close to the new stand on the North side of the River. Work should be completed for the start of the 2024/25 season with Fulham in the Premiership of the English Football League. The YouTube title is

Fulham FC Riverside Stand WIP at side of River Thames 19 May 2021

Date viewed:

Continuing my walk I approached Hammersmith Bridge knowing that it is closed to all traffic and pedestrians. In addition I had to walk a short detour because walkers are not allowed to walk under the end of the bridge which is over the path. As I am writing in July 2024 I have learned that the bridge has temporarily re-opened to cyclists, cargo bikes and e-scooters. They have created a new two-way central lane across the bridge to allow greater access to residents, visitors and businesses on both sides of the river. Spanning three metres wide, the cycle lane is likely to remain open for around 10 weeks. This means cyclists will no longer have to dismount and walk their bikes across, which frees up the footways for pedestrians. The delays have continued for a variety of reasons and I doubt that it will be fully functional for a few years yet. The title of my YouTube video is

Hammersmith Bridge London-Total Closure Michael Parkinson walks detour May 2021

Date viewed:

In June 2021 I walked in the rural setting of South Nottinghamshire and witnessed something I had never seen before. It was extremely hot and two horses were licking each other. Because there was just an electric fence between the path I was walking along and the horses I was able to video close up. It appears this is a common practice when horses are 'turned out together' as they were in the field where I saw them. I hoped someone would post a comment but although the video has received nearly 1400 views and 8 likes in the three years since I loaded it, no one has obliged. The YouTube title is

Horses licking each other near Widmerpool, Nottinghamshire

Date viewed:

I have to confess to a smidgen of nepotism here because during the Covid outbreak of 2020 my daughter Julie was running an online choir. I asked her if I could include details in this book and this is her reply. 'I started an on line choir called Who Dares Sings during the Covid pandemic with people I'd been previously meeting at a community group. The idea was to use the Skype meetings to sing some uplifting songs to bring some joy into what was a difficult time for many people. The song Spread a Little Happiness had the perfect lyrics for the purpose of the choir, but we really only needed the chorus, it worked perfectly as a short introductory song to start the choir sessions. Luckily, I'd formed the choir with help from Nathan Tootill who is a talented musician and he was able to play the chorus on the keyboard. The method of broadcasting the music and lyrics to the choir members was through YouTube. We needed to be able to use Nathan's video in the same manner. I asked my Dad if he could help because I knew he'd been putting videos on YouTube for years and knew a lot more about it than me. He excelled in writing an explanatory piece for us and incorporating the video of Nathan playing the keyboard. By uploading it to YouTube it meant I could add the video to the playlist of each week's session'. That explanation tells the story perfectly, the title of the video that I loaded to YouTube is

Spread a Little Happiness, With Who Dares Sings

Date viewed:

Chapter 11

Scarborough Spa to Brighton Marathon

Joan and I have been visiting Scarborough and attending concerts performed by the Spa Orchestra since 2003. We usually stay for a week and attend every Spa concert during our holiday. The orchestra consists of ten musicians and is led from the piano by Musical Director Paul Laidlaw. Scarborough is the only seaside place to have their own professional orchestra. Morning concerts take place in the Suncourt, which is outdoors but sheltered from the wind by a construction of stone pillars and huge glass panels. In inclement weather morning concerts take place under cover in the Spa where the evening concerts are held. Sometimes it starts to rain during the morning and the musicians have to move indoors at the interval. You can see an example of this by looking at a video which I loaded to YouTube in 2017, the title is

> Scarborough Spa Orchestra, Suncourt to Grand Hall, Rain

Date viewed:

A digital piano is used for outdoor concerts but a full size acoustic instrument is situated inside the Grand Hall where evening concerts are held. Many other events take place in the Grand Hall throughout the year and the Spa Orchestra perform a New Year's Day concert there as well. Children are catered for with a 'Teddy Bears Picnic' concert each week. They are devised by Kathy Seabrook, the flautist with the Orchestra. Whilst these concerts are primarily for children, adults also attend. When we attended one we found it interesting watching Kathy trying to encourage the children to be interested but at the same time discouraging them from swarming all over the stage. The Spa Orchestra play a varied selection of popular light classical music. I have videoed a programme to indicate the sort of things they play. The YouTube title is

Scarborough Spa Orchestra, Sound clip & Programme 19 July 21

Date viewed:

On the 4th of August 2021 the National Anthems of India and England were played as players and officials of both teams stood respectfully on the field before play commenced. The occasion was the Cricket Test Match at Trent Bridge, Nottingham and this was followed by Jerusalem which has been adopted by the England team. India were in a good position to win the match but rain prevented play on the final day to the relief of England supporters. The title of the video I loaded to YouTube is

India & England National Anthems plus Jerusalem at Trent Bridge Test Match 4 Aug 2021

Date viewed:

On 7 December 2016 I went to the Noel Coward Theatre box office in the hope of finding a cheap ticket for 'Half a Sixpence' and got a bargain at £20. It was second from the gangway, front row of the stalls for the afternoon show but warned it was very close to the stage with restricted view. On arrival I spoke to people around me who all appeared to have seen the show many times and were enthusiastic about it especially the performance of Charlie Stemp. I received permission to video posters and screens showing clips from the show and did this before the show and during the interval. I loved the show and devised my spoken review combined with video clips the following day. You can see and hear what I achieved by looking at my YouTube video title

Half a Sixpence, Review by Michael Parkinson

Date viewed:

During April 2022 we enjoyed a holiday at Brighton and stayed at a Hotel on the seafront in Hove. There were loads of posters advertising the Brighton marathon so I decided to video the runners. I videoed near the eighteen miles point outside the Princess Marine Hotel so about eight miles from the end. The total distance of the Brighton marathon is 26.2 miles so the runners were very tired when they passed Joan and me. Some looked totally exhausted and I wondered if they were causing themselves physical harm. The well trained runners came past first followed by the less experienced ones with some in fancy dress. Some first aid people were close to us and they sometimes picked out runners who needed help. Whilst writing this story in July 2024 I noticed the video has received 1183 views with 17 likes and five comments from runners who had seen themselves and appreciated me posting to YouTube. I obtained the names and times of the top placed male and female runners and put them in the video information. The YouTube title is

Brighton Marathon, 10 April 2022 Close up of runners near 18 mile point

Date viewed:

Chapter 12

Mary Poppins to Steinway Teddy Bear

Joan and I went to see the musical 'Mary Poppins' at the Prince Edward Theatre, London on 21 October 2021. I was given permission to video in the Theatre before and after the show but obviously not while the show was running. Young twin girls, Ella and Daisy, with Mother were taken to the show as a surprise by their Father and they gave permission to include my chat with them in my review. The show was dazzlingly brilliant with Zizi Strallen and Charlie Stemp playing the leading roles. Singing, speaking, dancing, orchestra and flying was accomplished. Petula Clark is remembered by many and sang Feed the Birds.

Mary Poppins, London, Starring Charlie Stemp Oct 2021. Michael Parkinson Review
Date viewed:

In November 2021 Joan and I enjoyed a week at the Blakeney Hotel in Norfolk and went to a matinee performance of the Thursford Christmas Spectacular. The show includes over one hundred singers, dancers, musicians and speciality acts. Phil Kelsall, celebrated his 40th season playing the Wurlitzer Organ that year. During the remainder of the year Phil is principal organist at the Blackpool Tower Ballroom where he has completed his 44th season. He has performed internationally and made numerous recordings and received an MBE in 2010 for services to music. It is interesting to me that whilst playing at Thursford he meticulously follows the score and conductor whilst concentrating on his role of accompanying the other musicians. This is in complete contrast to his solo acts where he performs at fantastic speed and skill without written music. The

YouTube title is

> Phil Kelsall MBE achieves 40th season at Thursford Christmas Spectacular, 2021

Date viewed:

I spilt tea into the vent of my Peugeot 508 car by using the pull out drink holder. This resulted in the display screen not working properly. The Multi Function screen includes radio and route finding information, clock and much more. It comes on as normal on starting the car after it has not been used for about two hours but goes off after about an hour, driving or when going over bumps. The screen was taken out in March 2022 and the Radio was taken out and sent away for testing. The Radio was refitted after one week but the fault was not resolved. In May 2022 the Display Panel was taken out again and was sent away for testing. It was refitted ten days later but the fault was still not rectified. This is a video of Paul from One 2 One Car Audio Ltd re-fitting the screen on the second occasion. I emphasise that Paul has done his best and not charged me the full price for what he has done because the problem has not been fixed. Paul agreed to be videoed re-fitting the panel and for this story to be included in my book. The YouTube title is

> Display Screen Fitted in Peugeot 508 Car after tea spillage

Date viewed:

I will never understand why some YouTube videos attract viewing figures out of all proportion to the content. On 21 April 2022 I travelled from my home near Nottingham to the grave of Billy Fury which is situated in Westminster Mill Hill Cemetery, North London. I decided to make video of the journey from Kings Cross underground station to the grave to help people who wanted to visit. I made over 60 video clips which I used, the following day, to make four videos which I loaded to YouTube.

The YouTube titles were

> London Underground, Piccadilly Line, Kings Cross to Bounds Green

Date viewed:

London Bus 221, Bounds Green to Salcombe Gardens, Mill Hill

Date viewed:

Billy Fury Grave, Walk from 221 Bus Stop, Salcombe Gardens, Mill Hill

Date viewed:

Billy Fury, Graveside Tribute, by Michael Parkinson April 2022

Date viewed:

The video of the walk from the Salcombe Gardens bus stop to the grave is not particularly inspiring as it was 'Wheelie Bin' day and they were scattered all over the place on Milespit Hill. It finished with a brief clip of the grave. To my amazement the viewing figures for that video escalated dramatically and the figure is now 51,288. The objective of my visit was to speak a tribute at the grave. This has achieved 1478 views at the time of writing which is normal. The underground journey has attracted 262 views with 368 looking at the 221 Bus from Bounds Green to Salcombe Gardens.

When Amy started work at Steinway during February 2013 she noticed that a Teddy Bear had been thrown into the waste bin. It was a dirty looking thing with a drab Navy Blue Jacket and she was told that it was not wanted. Amy rescued the Bear, cleaned it up and put it on her desk. I noticed the Bear some time later and suggested to Amy that I could ask a friend to make some clothing for it and to embroider the Steinway Logo. My friend knitted the jumper, did the embroidery and I took it in on Wednesday 17 April. The Steinway Staff, George, Maura and Amy were delighted to see the result of the craftsmanship and we did a humorous presentation. The YouTube title is

Steinway Teddy Bear, Rescued by Amy

Date viewed:

The Bear became something of an attraction at the Steinway Showroom situated at 44 Marylebone Lane, London WIU 2DB (Just off Oxford Street). Many visitors to Steinway admired the Bear on Amy's desk and enjoyed some fun remarks about it. On another visit to Steinway I met a man who was a good pianist and I asked him to play 'The Teddy Bears Picnic' whilst I videoed, he obliged and included some improvisations. His wife performed a little dance as I videoed. The YouTube video is

Teddy Bear Picnic Fun at Steinway, London, Paul Davies

Date viewed:

Chapter 13

Scarborough Bus to Shepherds Hut

In July 2023 Joan and I were enjoying our annual pilgrimage to Scarborough where we use the South Cliff Lift on our way to attend concerts played by the Scarborough Spa Orchestra. Another attraction is travelling on the open top bus from South Bay, passing the harbour and going along the bumpy road to Peasholme Park in the North Bay. The buses are very old but are enjoyed by thousands of holiday makers. The YouTube title is

> Scarborough, Open top Bus Ride from South to North Bay

Date viewed:

In October 2022 we booked into the Swan Hotel at Staines which enjoys an ideal position on the South bank of the River Thames. It is an ideal base for walking along the Thames Path towards Windsor in the East or by crossing Staines Bridge and walking towards Laleham in a Westerly direction. There are buses to various places from Staines Bus Station but you often feel as though it is necessary to lower your head because of low flying aircraft landing or taking off from Heathrow Airport. The nearest Piccadilly Line underground station is Hatton Cross and we got a number 203 bus to Staines Bus Station when we travelled there, a journey that takes about 45 minutes. We needed to get buses that went over Staines Bridge to get to the Swan Hotel. My YouTube video title is

> Swan Hotel at Staines upon Thames by Michael Parkinson

Date viewed:

On the first morning we walked to Staines Bridge and then walked back, past, the Swan Hotel and got to the Railway Bridge and the Boatyard. We then walked back to the Hotel and enjoyed a drink. That was a great achievement for Joan because she is not able to walk far. Here is the YouTube title that shows us taking that little walk

Staines Bridge walk to Boat Club and Swan Hotel, Joan & Michael Parkinson

Date viewed:

I noticed a Sikh wearing ceremonial dress whilst walking across Staines Bridge and met him later at the Swan Hotel. I asked if I could video an interview with him and he agreed. The YouTube title is

Sikh explains Ceremonial Dress, Articles of Faith to Michael Parkinson

Date viewed:

On Sunday 16 October 2022 I walked from the Swan Hotel, crossed Staines Bridge and walked along the Thames Path to Laleham. It was a pleasant walk and I saw many people running past me in both directions. As I approached Laleham I noticed a small control point at which the runners were turning round and running back in the direction they had come. Some of the runners looked fit and stylish but others looked extremely laboured and I thought some of them could be causing physical damage to themselves. I am too old to run so just enjoyed my steady walk with frequent stops to make video clips that I used on my return home to make a video for YouTube loading. In this case, the YouTube Title is

Staines Bridge, to Laleham. Walk with Michael Parkinson

Date viewed:

Having finished my walk just beyond Laleham I retraced my steps and walked back to Staines where I saw a large control area for the runners I had seen. I spoke to Lottie who is one of the leaders of the running club and was able to make my point about some of the runners not looking very fit. The YouTube title is

My YouTube Adventures

> Saturn Running Club. Staines Bridge, Lottie talks to Michael Parkinson

Date viewed:

Whilst staying at the Swan Hotel Joan and I had planned to achieve our ambition to ride on the cable car which goes over the Thames at Greenwich. We went to Staines bus Station, then the 203 bus to Hatton Cross and travelled on the London underground to North Greenwich Jubilee Line Station. We walked out of the station and made our way to the London Cable Car Terminal. Because we are seniors we only had to pay £5 each which we thought was very reasonable and we loved the experience. You can see how much we enjoyed it by looking at this YouTube title

> Cable Car over Thames at Greenwich. An interesting tourist attraction by Michael Parkinson

Date viewed:

The next part of fantastic touristy day was to travel on a driverless Docklands Light Railway journey from Tower Gateway to Becton. Fortunately there was not one of those annoying little boys who like to sit at the front and pretend to be the driver. So, I was able to do it. I drove this driverless Docklands Light Railway train from Tower Gateway to Becton. I stopped at Shadwell, Limehouse, Westferry, Poplar, Black Wall, East India, Canning Town, Royal Victoria, Custom House, Prince Regent, Royal Albert, Becton Park, Cyprus, Gallions Reach, and Becton. I edited out the time waiting at stations so please don't try to get off.

You can see how good my driving was by looking at this YouTube title

> Docklands Light Railway, Driver Michael Parkinson, Tower Gateway to Becton

Date viewed:

We then went into Central London and enjoyed a dinner at the John Lewis store in Oxford Street. We went up to the Roof Garden where Joan videoed. It is a delightful experience. The YouTube title is

John Lewis, London Oxford Street Roof Garden Video by Joan

Date viewed:

We went down the escalators walked the short distance to the Steinway Showroom and enjoyed a piano recital sponsored by the Keyboard Trust. When the concert finished we were forced to drink some lovely wine accompanied by nibbles. Because I would not be driving later in the evening (as is usually the case when I go to Steinway) I was able to have a couple of glasses. We then got on the underground and made our way back to Hatton Cross and on a bus to Staines Bus Station. We arrived there at around 11pm and all the buses had stopped running so we had to get a Taxi back to the Swan Hotel. It was the end of a lovely day and we were both exhausted but happy.

On 23 October 2022 I was walking along the Thames Path from the Swan Hotel and was going past Runnymede Boatyard. I stopped to look at a piece of machinery. A man from the Boatyard spoke to me and explained how they use what he told me was a Sheet Metal Folder. We chatted fo a couple of minutes and I told him that I was a YouTuber and liked to video unusual things. He invited me into the workshop and showed me a Shepherds Hut, that he and his colleague were building. It was very interesting and you can see it by looking at this YouTube title

Shepherds Hut Building by Emile and Martyn, The Wagon Workshop

Date viewed:

Chapter 14
Thames Path Walk

In Spring 2014 I walked from Blackfriars Bridge in London to Chelsea Bridge along the Thames Path. I had been going to London on most Wednesdays for many years and attended various concerts or just used buses and walked around places of interest. I enjoyed that walk so the following week I walked from Chelsea Bridge to Putney Bridge. The following week I used the buses from St Pancras to Putney and walked from Putney Bridge to Chiswick and used buses to get back to St Pancras Station for my homeward journey to Keyworth near Nottingham. My next walk involved buses to Chiswick Bridge and the walk to Mortlake which marks the end of the Oxford/Cambridge boat race course. I was finding it increasingly difficult to get to and from the starting and finishing points of my walks because obviously the distance from St Pancras Station was increasing. I was enjoying the challenge though so by the Autumn of 2014 I had reached Windsor but was still able to come back to Hyde Park Corner by bus and another one to St Pancras.

The following year, 2015, I decided to continue walking the Thames Path but had to use rail, buses and in some cases taxis as well to reach my starting and finishing points. This was expensive but it enhanced my enjoyment of the experience. The first walk that year was from Windsor to Maidenhead followed by subsequent arrivals at Bourne End, then Henley, Reading, Goring, Wallingford and Shillingford where I arrived in late September 2015. My journeys were becoming more time consuming so I was actually starting the walks later in the day and having to allow more time to get back to St Pancras for my 10pm train back to Nottingham.

In May 2016 I travelled to Shillingford in Oxfordshire to walk to Culham Bridge and my next walk was from Culham Bridge to Oxford followed by Oxford to Bablock Hythe where the river was becoming narrower but still wide and deep enough for small boats. The next walk was from Bablock Hythe to the beautifully named Tadpole Bridge. The next walk was from Tadpole Bridge to Lechlade followed by Lechlade to Cricklade which I did not reach. I was only about a mile from Cricklade (where I had arranged to phone the taxi) when the Thames Path grassy walk was blocked by a five barred wooden gate with a BULL IN FIELD sign. My dilemma was that I had not seen anyone for at least an hour so going back was not feasible whilst there was a wire mesh fence with barbed wire alongside the river to my left. I knew that there was a bridge over the River somewhere along that field but I did not know how far away it was. I decided to walk along the edge of the field to achieve the safety of the bridge and Cricklade where I could call my taxi. The field to my right sloped steeply upwards and I could not see any cattle in the field. I had walked about 400 yards along the path when I saw some cows and a huge bull which started to move towards me as it saw me. I turned round and hurried back towards the gate. A quick look over my shoulder showed that the bull had stopped walking towards me. I reached the safety of the gate, climbed over it and reviewed my situation. I decided to walk back towards the last road that I had seen about an hour before but after a short distance I spotted a clutch of cottages at the side of a narrow lane. I decided that if I could reach a cottage I would knock on the door and ask the occupant to give me the location so that I could phone my taxi from there. I did what I should not do and walked away from the path, down a field towards the little lane and spotted a large farmhouse on the other side of a thick, high, hawthorne hedge. I continued along the side of the big hedge and noticed a small gap with a drive leading to a gate and the lane beyond. I scrambled through the gap and walked to the gate which I climbed over and turned right along the lane towards the cottages. I knocked on the door of the only one that showed signs of life and a lady opened the door. She readily agreed to give the location so I could call my taxi which I immediately did. The lady invited me inside to wait but I declined because I wanted to wait for the taxi at the front gate. After a few minutes I heard the sound of a car close by but it did not arrive. The lady came out of the house just as my phone rang with the taxi driver saying he could not find my location. The lady spoke to the driver and confirmed where we were and she asked how I had got from the Bull in Field sign. She was shocked when I told her about scrambling through the hedge and said the landowner must have been out with the dogs and added that the dogs would have ripped me to pieces had they been there. The taxi arrived and sped me to Cricklade Station where I got on a train bound for Paddington. This was the worst experience of the whole walk and I was relieved to reach St Pancras Station with two minutes to spare for the 10pm train back to Nottingham.

The next week I walked from Cricklade back to the where I had seen the Bull in Field signs and noticed that I had only been about 200 yards from the safety of a bridge so it would have been better to have continued towards the bridge when I saw the bull. I reported the incident to Cricklade Town Council because I believe it is wrong that a farmer can put a BULL IN FIELD sign over the Thames Path Walk. The Council informed me a couple of weeks later that the landowner was completely within the law provided that there was actually a bull in the field. If such a sign had been put there without a bull being in the field the landowner would be liable for prosecution. I then walked back to Cricklade and on to Ashton Keynes. The following week my walk was from Ashton Keynes to Ewen. With the next walk being from Ewen to the source at Kemble on 17 August 2016. I arrived at the heap of stones signifying the source of the Thames but as it was August there was no water there. A few yards from the heap of stones there is a large granite stone inscribed with the words

THE CONSERVATORS OF THE RIVER THAMES 1857 to 1974

THIS STONE WAS PLACED HERE TO MARK THE SOURCE OF THE RIVER THAMES
Next to the stone is a wooden post with two finger posts with the words
THAMES PATH Public Footpath
THAMES BARRIER LONDON 184 MILES 294 KM

Having reached the source of the River Thames when it was dry I formed an ambition to return in wet winter conditions to video water at the source.

I realised that I had not walked the whole of the Thames Path because I had not walked from the Greenwich Barrier to Blackfriars Bridge so achieved that objective during the next few weeks. In late August 2016 I walked from the Thames Barrier to Greenwich and on the same date walked from Greenwich to Canary Wharf. On 31 August 2016 I walked along the Thames Path from Canary Wharf to Blackfriars Bridge thereby completing all 184 miles of the Thames Path.

On 11 March 2020 I realised my ambition to video water at the source of the River Thames and the streams running down the meadows to Kemble Bridge. I created many video clips of every walk and edited them when I was at home and loaded a video to YouTube.

These are titles of my Thames Path Walk videos loaded to my channel Michael notthatone Parkinson

Thames Source with water to Kemble   Thames Path Michael Parkinson

Date viewed:

___

Thames Barrier to Greenwich   Thames Path Michael Parkinson

Date viewed:

___

Greenwich to Canary Wharf   Thames Path Michael Parkinson

Date viewed:

___

Canary Wharf to Blackfriars Bridge   Thames Path Michael Parkinson

Date viewed:

___

Blackfriars to Chelsea Bridge   Thames Path Michael Parkinson

Date viewed:

___

Chelsea to Putney Bridge   Thames Path Michael Parkinson

Date viewed:

___

Putney to Mortlake   Thames Path Michael Parkinson

Date viewed:

___

        Mortlake to Richmond Bridge   Thames Path Michael Parkinson

Date viewed:

        Richmond to Hampton Bridge   Thames Path Michael Parkinson

Date viewed:

        Hampton Bridge to Elmbridge   Thames Path Michael Parkinson

Date viewed:

        Elmbridge to Shepperton   Thames Path Michael Parkinson

Date viewed:

        Thames Ferry Nauticalia   Thames Path Michael Parkinson

Date viewed:

        Weybridge to Shepperton   Thames Path Michael Parkinson

Date viewed:

        Pike caught in Thames at Shepperton   Thames Path Michael Parkinson

Date viewed:

        Shepperton to Staines   Thames Path Michael Parkinson

Date viewed:

Staines to Windsor   Thames Path Michael Parkinson

Date viewed:

Windsor to Maidenhead   Thames Path Michael Parkinson

Date viewed:

Maidenhead to Bourne End   Thames Path Michael Parkinson

Date viewed:

Bourne End to Henley   Thames Path Michael Parkinson

Date viewed:

Henley to Reading   Thames Path Michael Parkinson

Date viewed:

Reading to Goring   Thames Path Michael Parkinson

Date viewed:

Goring to Wallingford   Thames Path Michael Parkinson

Date viewed:

Wallingford to Shillingford   Thames Path Michael Parkinson

Date viewed:

Stonemason Thames Bargeman talks to Michael Parkinson
Date viewed:

Shillingford to Culham Bridge   Thames Path Michael Parkinson
Date viewed:

Culham Bridge to Oxford   Thames Path Michael Parkinson
Date viewed:

Oxford to Bablock Hythe   Thames Path Michael Parkinson
Date viewed:

Bablock Hythe to Tadpole Bridge   Thames Path Michael Parkinson
Date viewed:

Tadpole Bridge to Lechlade   Thames Path Michael Parkinson
Date viewed:

Lechlade to Cricklade, Bull notice   Thames Path Michael Parkinson
Date viewed:

Bull obstructs Thames Path near Cricklade   Thames Path Michael Parkinson
Date viewed:

Cricklade to Water Eaton, Bull gone   Thames Path Michael Parkinson

Date viewed:

Cricklade to Ashton Keynes   Thames Path Michael Parkinson

Date viewed:

Ashton Keynes to Ewen   Thames Path Michael Parkinson

Date viewed:

Ewen to Source   Thames Path Michael Parkinson

Date viewed:

Chapter 15

Christmas Day in the Workhouse to Scottish Army in Trafalgar Square

When I was a boy I acquired a book with the title in, capital letters, 'THE DAGONET AND OTHER POEMS' it was written by George Robert Sims and published in 1903 by George Routledge & Sons Limited. I particularly liked 'It was Christmas Day in the Workhouse' and 'Billy's Rose'. In 1998, I made a VHS video film of a young lady reading two of the ballads and poetry and called it 'Then and Now'. I included the Victorian ballads to represent 'Then' and poetry written by local writers to depict 'Now'. When I became a YouTuber I transferred some of the work to YouTube where it can still be seen. The first YouTube title is

    Christmas Day in the Workhouse, Victorian Ballad, read by Hayley Griffin

Date viewed:

The link to the second is

    Billy's Rose Victorian Ballad, Read by Hayley Griffin, G,R Sims

Date viewed:

When I originally asked Hayley to read the ballads I expected her to be terrified and needing a lot of training. Instead, she nonchalantly replied 'Oh I know them, my Mother is a teacher and I have been familiar with them since I was an infant'. Here is Hayley introducing the video

> Hayley Griffin, Introduction to Then and Now

Date viewed:

When she was younger she had broken her leg and was taken to the Nottingham Goose Fair in a wheelchair. The reaction she experienced motivated her to write this poem which was printed in the Nottingham Evening Post dated 9 February 1998. Here is the YouTube title

> Seen But Not Heard (Confined to a Wheelchair) Written and read by Hayley Griffin

Date viewed:

Richard Phipps wrote a poem describing a fish riding a bicycle and I believe every word of it, Here is the YouTube title

> Fish riding a bicycle, Hayley Griffin reads Selwyn McGrigger

Date viewed:

In September 2010 I was working on my promotion of a Billy Fury Dance Show which was eventually performed at the Palace Theatre, Mansfield on 8 October 2011. The format of my show involved selected dancers from four amateur dance academies telling the Billy Fury Story and performing choreographed routines to his sound recordings. I asked Vince Eager to speak a tribute to Billy Fury in the show and he agreed. This was confirmed by letter and I agreed a fee with Vince. However, a few weeks before the date of the show I received and message from Vince stating that his agent had booked for another gig on the date of my show. He offered to do something to make amends so I suggested that he speak about Billy whilst I videoed so that I could put it on YouTube and he agreed. I set up a makeshift recording studio in my garage and Vince obliged. He spoke about the famous audition where young Ronald Wycherley met Larry Parnes at the Birkenhead Essoldo and Ron was put on stage that night. You can see and hear Vince on YouTube title

Billy Fury by Vince Eager, Audition at Birkenhead Essoldo

Date viewed:

During March 2024 Joan and I had to set up the British Telecom voice adapter system and were concerned about how to do it. We read the instructions but were not very confident that we understood them properly. I decided to video our experience and made a video (with a lot of editing) which I loaded to YouTube. My idea was that if two doddering old people could set it up then anyone could do it. I loaded the video to YouTube on 2 March 2024 and six months later, on 15 September, it has achieved 11,755 views, 75 likes and 37 comments. The YouTube title is

BT Digital Voice Adapter, how two old people set it up

Date viewed:

On 6 February 2012 I attended a concert at St James's Church Piccadilly and was so impressed with the performance of Hannah Lewis, playing cello, that I promoted a concert for her in Nottingham. This took place on 28 June 2012 at the Djanogly Recital Hall, Lakeside Arts Centre, University Park, Nottingham. The theme of my concert was 'Music and Romance' and included Erika Zeckser Owen, *viola* and Mitra Alice Tham, *piano*.

Erika lives near Nottingham but I had to meet Mitra and Hannah (with her cello) at Loughborough Station and drive them to the Recital Hall. We called at our house on the way so the musicians could get established in our spare room where they stayed the night. I noticed that Hannah practiced non stop from her arrival at the Recital Hall until it was time to change for her first half performance of Chopin's Polonaise Brilliante Opus 3. She then continually practiced until her second half performance of Franz Liszt's Liebestraum (Loves Dreams number 3). The concert was a great success and particularly gruelling for Mitra Alice Tham, *piano,* she was on stage for every minute of the concert, playing her own solo pieces and accompanying Erika and Hannah. After the concert had finished Joan and I went home with our guests and enjoyed a snack and drinks before going to bed. The following morning Joan presented a continental breakfast but Hannah asked if she could see the video that I had made of her part in the concert. We therefore enjoyed our breakfast whilst watching the relevant parts of the performance from the previous night. To my relief Hannah expressed her satisfaction and gave me permission to load it to YouTube. Soon afterwards we got into the car and I drove to Loughborough Railway Station where Mitra and Hannah boarded the train to London with the cello and their luggage.

I have selected three YouTube titles from this concert

Chopin Fantaise Impromptu, Piano, I'm Always Chasing Rainbows, Mitra Alice Tham
Date viewed:

Liszt Liebestraum, Hannah Lewis cello Mitra Alice Tham piano
Date viewed:

Max Bruch, Romanze for Viola, Erika Zeckser Owen, Mitra Alice Tham, Piano
Date viewed:

On Wednesday 14 August 2013 I had travelled by train to London and was making my way to St James's Church, Piccadilly to attend the lunchtime concert. I had boarded a bus at St Pancras which was bound for Trafalgar Square and planned to walk across the Square which was usually very quite. As the bus was nearing its destination outside Charing Cross mainline station I heard and saw a huge commotion, footballs being kicked into the air and loads of blue shirted Scotland football supporters. After I had got off the bus and started to walk across the square I heard the sound of bagpipes being played and my YouTuber mind clicked in. I jostled myself into a position where I could video the bagpipes and a family of black people appeared in front of me. The parents were enjoying the scene but the children were not too keen at first but gradually threw off their inhibitions and began moving to the music. I videoed the scene and when I arrived at St James's I sat at the back of the Church and loaded it to YouTube. I made up a very dramatic title and by the time the concert finished noticed that It had achieved a lot of views. As I write, in September 2024, the view count is 28,522 with 92 likes and 37 comments. I appealed for people to supply the names of tunes and performers, which they did, enabling me to include them into the description. This was an example of a me taking advantage of an unexpected opportunity that presented itself. The YouTube title is

> Scottish Army Invade Trafalgar Square, Bagpipes Drums Aug 2013

Date viewed:

CHAPTER 16

NOTTINGHAM ORGAN SOCIETY

INTRODUCTION & YEAR 2013

I went to a Nottingham Organ Society concert at the Bonington Theatre at Arnold in July 2008 and enlisted as a member because I enjoyed it so much. The society was founded in 1967 to cater for people who are interested in music played on electric organs and keyboards. Concerts usually take place on the first Monday of the Month but this does vary because of Bank Holidays or unusual circumstances. We are fortunate to use the Bonington Theatre at Arnold which has comfortable raked seating with good lighting and technical facilities. There is a large car park with free parking after 6pm, just right for the evening concerts that start at 7-30pm.

The society own a system of cameras and screens that enable the audience to see fingers on keys and feet on the pedals from all seating positions. In 2024 the theatre technician has used an alternative system to achieve the same result without the clutter of wires and equipment on stage. Michael Carpenter, a member of the society produces 'Harmony' a publication that is posted to members of the group timed to arrive a few days before each concert. In 2013 I began videoing some of the performances and loading videos to YouTube. Howard Beaumont was the first performer I videoed. My position at the side of the stage was not ideal because the sound was not balanced properly. I learned that it is better recorded from the front row of the theatre and positioned myself in the front row for subsequent recordings.

The following chapters show titles of music which have been put on to YouTube channel name Michael notthatone Parkinson. This name was used to avoid confusion with Sir Michael Parkinson who sadly died in 2023. It is not a comprehensive list of all the concerts because some organists do not allow their work to be loaded to YouTube.

Here are the titles of the first two experimental videos loaded to YouTube.

Bach to Beatles, Howard Beaumont, Nottm Organ Society 7 Jan 2013

Date viewed:

Persian Market, Howard Beaumont, Nottm Organ Society 7 Jan 2013

Date viewed:

Dirkjan Ranzijn performed the November 2013 concert. Here are YouTube titles loaded on 5 Nov 2013

Dirkjan Ranzijn, Party Time Paloma Blanca, Dog in Audience

Date viewed:

Dirkjan Ranzijn, If I Never Sing Another Song, Nottingham Organ Society

Date viewed:

Dirkjan Ranzijn, Saturday Night Fever, Nottingham Organ Society

Date viewed:

Dirkjan Ranzijn, Come Share The Wine, Nottingham Organ Society

Date viewed:

Dirkjan Ranzijn, Beautiful Sunday, Nottingham Organ Society

Date viewed:

Dirkjan Ranzijn, YMCA, Nottingham Organ Society

Date viewed:

Dirkjan Ranzijn, Lady in Red, Nottingham Organ Society

Date viewed:

Dirkjan Ranzijn, We are the Champions, (Queen), Nottingham Organ Society

Date viewed:

Dirkjan Ranzijn, Andrew Rieu, Snow Waltz, Nottingham Organ Society

Date viewed:

Dirkjan Ranzijn, Only For One Day, Nottingham Organ Society

Date viewed:

Dirkjan Ranzijn, I Only Want To Be With You, Nottm Organ Society

Date viewed:

Dirkjan Ranzijn, Empty Chairs Empty Tables, Nottingham Organ Society

Date viewed:

Dirkjan Ranzijn, Falling in Love With You, Nottingham Organ Society

Date viewed:

Dirkjan Ranzijn, World Tour, Nottingham Organ Society

Date viewed:

Dirkjan Ranzijn, The Beginning, Nottingham Organ Society

Date viewed:

Dirkjan Ranzijn, Besame Mucho etc, Nottingham Organ Society

Date viewed:

Dirkjan Ranzijn, Sexy Camilla Story, Nottingham Organ Society

Date viewed:

Dirkjan Ranzijn, To Make You Feel My Love, Nottingham Organ

Date viewed:

Dirkjan Ranzijn, Viennese Style, Nottingham Organ Society

Date viewed:

Dirkjan Ranzijn, Lune de Parie, Nottingham Organ Society

Date viewed:

NOS Intro & Dirkjan Ranzijn, Marriage de Amour, Nottingham Organ Society

Date viewed:

Dirkjan Ranzijn, Leroy Brown, Nottingham Organ Society

Date viewed:

Dirkjan Ranzijn, Miracle Song, Nottingham Organ Society

Date viewed:

Dirkjan Ranzijn, Beautiful Noise, Tonight, Nottingham Organ Society

Date viewed:

Robert Wolfe performed the December 2013 concert. Here are the YouTube titles loaded on 4 December 2013

Robert Wolfe, West Side Story, Nottingham Organ Society

Date viewed:

Robert Wolfe, Christmas Medley, Nottingham Organ Society

Date viewed:

Robert Wolfe, Tiger Rag, Nottingham Organ Society

Date viewed:

Robert Wolfe, Hymns to My 'Gal' selection Nottingham Organ Society

Date viewed:

Robert Wolfe, Eleanora, Tico Tico to Sabre Dance, Nottm Organ Society

Date viewed:

Robert Wolfe Walking in the Air, Oh Holy Night Nottingham Organ Society

Date viewed:

Robert Wolfe, Moon River, Mancini Medley, Nottingham Organ Society

Date viewed:

Robert Wolfe, Mancini March, Brass Buttons, Nottingham Organ Society

Date viewed:

Chapter 17
Nottingham Organ Society – Year 2014

Mark Thompson performed the January 2014 concert. Here are You Tube titles loaded on 7 January 2014

    Mark Thompson, Crocodile Rock & More, Nottm Organ Society

Date viewed:

    Mark Thompson, Theatre-land, Jack Strachey, Nottingham Organ Society

Date viewed:

    Mark Thompson, A Nightingale Sang in Berkeley Square, Nottm OS

Date viewed:

    Mark Thompson, My Way, Nottingham Organ Society

Date viewed:

    Mark Thompson, Guess the Shows, Nottingham Organ Society

Date viewed:

Mark Thompson The Lonely Shepherd/James Last, Nottm Organ Society

Date viewed:

Mark Thompson, Tarantella Trio, Nottingham Organ Society

Date viewed:

Mark Thompson Fly me to the Moon, Nottingham Organ Society

Date viewed:

Mark Thompson, Washington Post etc, Nottingham Organ Society

Date viewed:

Mark Thompson, Classical Trio, Nottingham Organ Society

Date viewed:

Mark Thompson, Don't Get Around Much, Nottingham Organ Society

Date viewed:

Mark Thompson, Forgotten Dreams, Nottingham Organ Society

Date viewed:

Mark Thomson, Latin Medley. Nottingham Organ Society

Date viewed:

Mark Thompson, Five Finger Boogie, Tiger Rag, Nottm Organ Society

Date viewed:

Mark Thomson, Misty, Nottingham Organ Society

Date viewed:

Mark Thomson, Prelude Classic Style, Nottm Organ Society

Date viewed:

Mark Thompson, Take the A Train, Nottingham Organ Society

Date viewed:

Tim Flint performed the February 2014 concert. These are YouTube titles loaded on 4 February 2014

Comedians Gallop, Tim Flint, Nottingham Organ Society

Date viewed:

Muskrat Ramble, Tim Flint, Nottingham Organ Society

Date viewed:

Lover Variations, Tim Flint, Nottm Organ Society

Date viewed:

Wedding Samba, Tim Flint, Nottm Organ Society

Date viewed:

For Once in my Life, Tim Flint, Nottm Organ Society

Date viewed:

Your'e Too Wonderful, Tim Flint, Nottm Organ Society

Date viewed:

Mozart 40 Theme by Tim Flint, Nottm Organ Society

Date viewed:

Nearness of You, Tim Flint, Nottm Organ Society

Date viewed:

Bandology Tim Flint, Nottm Organ Society

Date viewed:

Vienna Style, Tim Flint, Nottm Organ Society

Date viewed:

Out of Africa, Tim Flint, Nottm Organ Society

Date viewed:

Portrait of a Flirt, Tim Flint, Nottm Organ Society

Date viewed:

Intermezzo Cavalleria Rusticano, Tim Flint, NOS

Date viewed:

Theatre Organ Medley. Tim Flint, Nottm Organ Society

Date viewed:

Summer Medley, Tim Flint, Nottm Organ Society

Date viewed:

Cheek to Cheek, Tim Flint, Nottm Organ Society

Date viewed:

Claire Greig performed the March 2014 concert. These are YouTube titles loaded on 4 March 2014

Eine Klein Nachtmusik, Claire Greig, Wersi Performer

Date viewed:

Orpheus in the Underworld, Claire Greig, Wersi Organ

Date viewed:

Dizzy Fingers, Claire Greig, Wersi Organ

Date viewed:

Claire by Claire Greig, Wersi Organ Gabriels Oboe

Date viewed:

Here There Everywhere (Beetles) Claire Greig, Wersi Organ

Date viewed:

Toccata, Widor, Claire Greig, Wersi Organ

Date viewed:

Klaus Wunderlich Medley, Claire Greig, Wersi Organ

Date viewed:

Out of Africa, Claire Greig, Wersi Organ

Date viewed:

Glen Miller Medley, Claire Greig, Wersi Organ

Date viewed:

Abba, Mama Mia Medley, Claire Greig, Wersi Organ

Date viewed:

Elton John Medley, Claire Greig, Wersi Organ

Date viewed:

Dream of Olwin, Claire Greig, Wersi Organ

Date viewed:

Dreaming Ballerina, Claire Greig, Wersi, Nottm Organ Society

Date viewed:

Arrival of the Queen of Sheba, Claire Greig, Wersi Organ

Date viewed:

Strauss Waltzes, Claire Greig, Wersi Organ

Date viewed:

Dancing Medley, Claire Greig, Wersi Organ

Date viewed:

Liberty Belle, Souza, Claire Greig, Wersi Organ

Date viewed:

Dam Busters March, Claire Greig, Organ

Date viewed:

Nicholas Martin performed another concert on 24 March because he was not able to perform in April.

These are YouTube titles loaded on 25 March 2014

You'll Never Walk Alone from Carousel, Nicholas Martin Organ

Date viewed:

Tiger Rag/Toccata mix, Nicholas Martin at Nottingham Organ Society

Date viewed:

Show Music Medley, Nicholas Martin, Organ

Date viewed:

Autism, Nicholas Martin speaks to Nottingham Organ Society

Date viewed:

Amparito Roca, Nicholas Martin, Nottingham Organ Society

Date viewed:

Phantom of Opera, Mamma Mia, Nicholas Martin, Organ

Date viewed:

Show Favourites, Nicholas Martin, Nottingham Organ Society

Date viewed:

Vienna to Cabaret medley, Nicholas Martin, organ

Date viewed:

Master of the House, Le Miserables medley, Nicholas Martin

Date viewed:

Twelfth Street Rag medley, Nicholas Martin organ

Date viewed:

Dance medley, Nicholas Martin, Nottm Organ Society

Date viewed:

Side Saddle, Mack the Knife, Nicholas Martin organ

Date viewed:

Chapter 18

Nottingham Organ Society – Year 2017

I did not video any concerts during years 2015 & /2016 and only videoed one concert during 2017.

Claire Greig performed the August 2017 concert. These are YouTube titles loaded on 8 August 2017.

    Mornings at Seven Claire Greig, Wersi, Nottm Organ Society

Date viewed:

    Die Fledermaus Overture, Claire Greig, Wersi, Nottm Organ Society

Date viewed:

    Barry Manilow Medley, Claire Greig, Nottm Organ Society

Date viewed:

    Mozart to Manilow mix, Claire Greig, Nottm Organ Society

Date viewed:

Dreaming Ballerina, Claire Greig, Wersi, Nottm Organ Society

Date viewed:

Tico Tico, Claire Greig, Wersi, Nottm Organ Society

Date viewed:

Gold, Spandau Ballet, Claire Greig, Wersi, Nottm Organ Society

Date viewed:

Lonely Shepherd, Claire Greig, Wersi, Nottm Organ Society

Date viewed:

Merry Christmas Mr Lawrence, Claire Greig, Wersi Organ

Date viewed:

Shadows Medley, Claire Greig, Wersi, Nottm Organ Society

Date viewed:

Beer Barrel Polka, Claire Greig, Wersi, Nottm Organ Society

Date viewed:

Circus Renz, Claire Greig, Wersi, Nottm Organ Society

Date viewed:

Irish Jig/Hoedown Claire Greig, Wersi, Nottm Organ Society

Date viewed:

Clarinet & Tritsch Polka, Claire Greig, Nottm Organ Society

Date viewed:

Rule the World, Claire Greig, Wersi, Nottm Organ Society

Date viewed:

Morning, Peer Gynt, Claire Greig, Wersi, Nottm Organ Society

Date viewed:

Klaus Wunderlich Medley, Claire Greig, Wersi, Nottm Organ

Date viewed:

Angela & Hill St Blues, Claire Greig, Wersi Organ NOS

Date viewed:

Roger Whittaker Medley, Claire Greig, Nottm Organ Society

Date viewed:

Take Five, Claire Greig, Wersi, Nottingham Organ Society

Date viewed:

St Louis Blues, Claire Greig, Wersi, Nottingham Organ Society

Date viewed:

Chapter 19
Nottingham Organ Society – Year 2018

Chris Stanbury performed the March 2018 Concert. These are the YouTube titles loaded

        1812 overture Tchaikovsky, Chris Stanbury, Nottm OS

Date viewed:

        Hot Toddy, East of the Sun, Chris Stanbury, Nottm OS

Date viewed:

        Bohemian Rhapsody, Chris Stanbury, Nottingham OS

Date viewed:

        Raindrops keep falling on my head, Chris Stanbury, NOS

Date viewed:

        Count Basie tribute, Corner Pocket, Chris Stanbury, NOS

Date viewed:

Sound of music medley, Chris Stanbury, Nottm OS

Date viewed:

On a Clear Day, Chris Stanbury, Nottingham Organ Society

Date viewed:

Dusty Springfield tribute, Chris Stanbury, Nottingham Organ Society

Date viewed:

At the sound of the Swinging Cymbal, Chris Stanbury, Nottm OS

Date viewed:

Raiders of the lost Ark, Chris Stanbury, Nottm Organ Society

Date viewed:

Lets Dance, Bobby's Girl, Sweet 16 etc, Chris Stanbury, Nottm OS

Date viewed:

Max Bygraves medley, Chris Stanbury, Nottingham Organ Society

Date viewed:

Children's favourites, Chris Stanbury, Nottingham Organ Society

Date viewed:

Swinging Shepherd Blues, Chris Stanbury, Nottm Organ Society

Date viewed:

Glen Miller medley played by Chris Stanbury, Nottm Organ Society

Date viewed:

Vienna City of my dreams, Chris Stanbury, Nottm Organ Society

Date viewed:

Thunder and Lightening Polka, Chris Stanbury, Nottm OS

Date viewed:

Stevie Wonder's Sunshine of my life, Chris Stanbury, Nottm OS

Date viewed:

Bugler's Holiday. Chris Stanbury, Nottingham Organ Society

Date viewed:

Tico Tico, Chris Stanbury, Nottingham Organ Society

Date viewed:

David Thomas performed the October 2018 concert. Here are the YouTube titles loaded.

Over the Rainbow Medley, Drawbar Magic, David Thomas, organ

Date viewed:

Besame Mucho & more, David Thomas, Nottingham Organ Society

Date viewed:

Fred & Ginger Tribute, David Thomas, Nottm Organ Society

Date viewed:

December 2018 was a unique Christmas event. Here are YouTube titles of varied entertainment

Rudolph the Red Nosed Reindeer, The whole cast, Christmas Variety Concert, NOS

Date viewed:

Santa Claus is coming to Town with Santa himself at Nottingham Organ Society

Date viewed:

White Christmas, The cast, Christmas Variety Concert, Nottingham Organ Society 2018

Date viewed:

Have Yourself a merry little Christmas, Jane & Mark Christmas Variety Concert, NOS

Date viewed:

Easy like Sunday morning, Jane & Mark, Christmas Variety Concert, NOS

Date viewed:

Make you feel my love, Jane and Mark, Christmas Variety Show, NOS

Date viewed:

Willie Wagglesticks Walkabout, Ei Lwin, piano, Christmas Variety Concert, NOS

Date viewed:

Silent Night, Major Oak Barber Shop Chorus, Nottm Organ Society

Date viewed:

Jingle Bells, Major Oak Barber Shop Chorus, Nottingham Organ Society

Date viewed:

Lion Sleeps Tonight, Major Oak Barber Shop Chorus, NOS

Date viewed:

June and Mark, Organ and Keyboard at Christmas Variety Concert NOS

Date viewed:

Dance, Winter Wonderland, NOS Christmas Variety Concert 2018

Date viewed:

Swing Low Sweet Chariot ,Major Oak Barber Shop Chorus, Nottm Organ Society

Date viewed:

Java Jive, Major Oak Barber Shop Chorus, Christmas Variety Concert NOS

Date viewed:

Phillip, Keyboard, Christmas Concert, Nottingham Organ Society 2018

Date viewed:

Chapter 20
Nottingham Organ Society – Year 2019

Phil Brown performed the September 2019 concert. Here are the YouTube titles loaded.

Amerillo, With You, Sugar, etc Phil Brown, Nottm Organ Society

Date viewed:

Adelene, Phil Brown, Bohm Organ, Nottingham Organ Society

Date viewed:

Second Waltz, Dmitri Shostakovich, Phil Brown on Bohm Organ

Date viewed:

Speed Your Journey, Phil Brown, Bohm Organ, Nottm Organ Society

Date viewed:

Tico Tico, played by Phil Brown, Nottingham Organ Society Sep 2019

Date viewed:

Circus Renz played by Phil Brown, Bohm Organ, Nottm Organ Society

Date viewed:

We'll Meet Again, Phil Brown Bohm Organ, Nottm Organ Society

Date viewed:

Nicholas Martin performed the November 2019 concert. Here are just two YouTube titles loaded.

Tiger Rag/Toccata mix, Nicholas Martin at Nottingham Organ Society

Date viewed:

Two Autistic children, Nicholas Martin. 'Miracles to Believe In'

Date viewed:

Dirkjan Ranzijn performed the December 2019 concert. Here are the YouTube titles loaded

Date viewed:

Sweet Caroline/Beautiful Noise, Dirk Jan Ranzijn at Nottingham Organ Society

Date viewed:

Les Miserable Medley, Dirk Jan Ranzijn, Nottingham Organ Society

Date viewed:

Lugano, Played and Composed by Dirk Jan Ranzijn at Nottingham Organ Society

Date viewed:

Viva Los Vegas, Dirk Jan Ranzijn at Nottingham Organ Society, Arnold

Date viewed:

Circus Music by Dirk Jan Ranzijn at Nottingham Organ Society, Arnold

Date viewed:

Perfect (Ed Sheeran) played by Dirk Jan Ranzijn at Nottingham Organ Society

Date viewed:

Taka Takata played by Dirk Jan Ranzijn at Nottingham Organ Society, Arnold

Date viewed:

One Man's Dream (Yanni) played by Dirk Jan Ranzijn, Nottm Organ Society

Date viewed:

Dirkjan Ranzijn, ambition to perform with André Rieu

Date viewed:

Shostakovich, Second Waltz, by Dirk Jan Ranzijn at Nottm Organ Society

Date viewed:

Chess, The Musical, Dirk Jan Ranzijn, Nottingham Organ Society, Arnold

Date viewed:

Obladi Oblada/Yellow Submarine, Dirk Jan Ranzijn at Nottingham Organ Society

Date viewed:

Dirk Jan Ranzijn, Music from Around the World for Nottingham Organ Society

Date viewed:

Morning in Cornwall (James Last) Dirk Jan Ranzijn at Nottm Organ Society

Date viewed:

Take Me Home Country Rose, Dirk Jan Ranzijn, Nottingham Organ Society

Date viewed:

Spirit of Norway, Composed/played, Dirk Jan Ranzijn, Nottingham Organ Society

Date viewed:

Despacito, Dirk Jan Ranzijn, Nottingham Organ Society, Bonington Theatre Arnold

Date viewed:

Vienna medley, Dirk Jan Ranzijn at Nottingham Organ Society, Arnold

Date viewed:

Never on Sunday, Dirk Jan Ranzijn at Nottingham Organ Society, Arnold
Date viewed:

Hallelujah, Dirk Jan Ranzijn, Nottingham Organ Society, Bonington Theatre, Arnold
Date viewed:

Let it Swing, Bobbysocks, Rock n Roll, Dirk Jan Ranzijn at Nottingham Organ Society
Date viewed:

Love is all I have to give, Dirk Jan Ranzijn at Nottingham Organ Society, Arnold
Date viewed:

December 2019 featured another Organ Society show. Here are the YouTube titles
Date viewed:

Oh Holy Night, Sung at the Nottingham Organ Society 2019 Christmas Concert
Date viewed:

Christmas medley of 1973 songs at Nottingham Organ Society concert 2019
Date viewed:

I Saw Mummy Kissing Santa Claus, Alan Wilson NOS 2019 Christmas concert
Date viewed:

Here There & Everywhere, Alan Wilson, Nottm Organ Society 2019 Christmas concert

Date viewed:

Norwegian Woods, Alan Wilson, Nottingham Organ Society 2019 Christmas concert

Date viewed:

Star Wars, Death Canteen at Nottingham Organ Society 2019 Christmas concert

Date viewed:

Freddie Feelgood Funky Four Piece Band, QM singers, NOS Christmas 2019 concert

Date viewed:

White Christmas, QM singers, Nottingham Organ Society 2019 Christmas concert

Date viewed:

Something, QM singers, Nottingham Organ Society 2019 Christmas concert

Date viewed:

Sinead dances 'What Christmas Means to Me' Nottingham Organ Society 2019 Christmas concert

Date viewed:

Magic, Record attempt at Bonington Theatre, Arnold in NOS 2019 Christmas concert

Date viewed:

Hey Jude, Trevor & Mark at Nottingham Organ Society 2019 Christmas concert

Date viewed:

One Step at a Time, Music Mark Everatt words Steve Cook, 2019 NOS Christmas concert

Date viewed:

Do You Hear What I Hear, OK singers at 2019 Nottingham Organ Society Christmas concert

Date viewed:

Sloop John B, OK singers, 2019 Nottingham Organ Society Christmas concert

Date viewed:

All My Loving, OK singers, Nottingham Organ Society 2019 Christmas concert

Date viewed:

My Christmas Wish, Alan Wilson, Nottingham Organ Society 2019 Christmas concert

Date viewed:

The Most Wonderful Time of the Year, Alan Wilson NOS 2019 Christmas concert

Date viewed:

Star Wars Darth Vader Assume Control of Arnold Bonington Theatre

Date viewed:

Chapter 21

Nottingham Organ Society – Year 2020

Brett Wales performed the February 2020 concert. Here are the three titles loaded to YouTube

    Dualing Banjos, Brett Wales at Nottingham Organ Society

Date viewed:

A Kind of Magic, (Queen) Brett Wales plays his version at Nottm Organ Society

Date viewed:

This Old House, Red River Valley, Rock Around Clock, Brett Wales, Wersi Organ

Date viewed:

Byron Jones performed the March 2020 concert. Here are the titles loaded to YouTube

Old Piano Rag preceded by mystery tune. Byron Jones, Nottm Organ Society March 2020

Date viewed:

Intermezzo, Softly awakes my heart, Chorus Hebrew Slaves, Byron Jones

Date viewed:

The Lost Chord, Byron Jones, Nottingham Organ Society

Date viewed:

Latin medley, Byron Jones, at Nottingham Organ Society

Date viewed:

All in the April Evening, Byron Jones, Nottingham Organ Society

Date viewed:

English Marches, Byron Jones at Nottingham Organ Society

Date viewed:

Welsh Marches, Byron Jones playing at Nottingham Organ Society

Date viewed:

Because of Covid no more concerts were performed in 2020

Chapter 22
Nottingham Organ Society – Year 2021

The Covid pandemic struck in Mid March 2020 so all concerts ceased and did not restart until September 2021, The next concert which I videoed was performed by Chris Powell on 6 September 2021. Here are the titles loaded to YouTube.

Last Night of Proms, Chris Powell, Nottm Organ Society, Sep 2021

Date viewed:

Sixties Favourites, Chris Powell, Nottingham Organ Society

Date viewed:

Show Memories Chris Powell at Nottingham Organ Society

Date viewed:

Morning In Cornwall James Last played by Chris Powell, Organ

Date viewed:

Buddy Holly Medley, Chris Powell, Nottingham Organ Society

Date viewed:

Elvis tunes, Now or Never, Falling in Love, Wonder of you, Chris Powell, Organ

Date viewed:

Blackpool Tower favourites by Chris Powell at Nottingham Organ Society

Date viewed:

Great Escape Film tune, Chris Powell Nottingham Organ Society

Date viewed:

Tom Jones tunes. Not unusual, Green Grass, Delilah, Chris Powell-Organ

Date viewed:

Make you feel my love (Adele) Chris Powell, Organ

Date viewed:

Orpheus and Can Can. Chris Powell playing Roland Atelier Organ

Date viewed:

Lennon:McCartney tunes, Chris Powell Roland Atelier organ

Date viewed:

Glen Miller medley Chris Powell plays Roland Atelier organ

Date viewed:

Gabriels Oboe by Ennio Morricone, Chris Powell, Nottm Organ Society

Date viewed:

Happy Music, James Last, Chris Powell, Nottingham Organ Society Sep 2021

Date viewed:

Nicholas Martin performed the December 2021 concert. Here are the titles loaded to YouTube

James Bond Theme, Nicholas Martin, Nottingham Organ Society

Date viewed:

Christmas Medley, Nicholas Martin, Nottm Organ Society Dec 21

Date viewed:

Christmas tunes, Nicholas Martin A Child is born etc, Nottm Organ Soc Dec 21

Date viewed:

Merry Christmas Everyone, Nicholas Martin, Nottm Organ Society Dec 2021

Date viewed:

Latin Rhythm Dance Medley, Nicholas Martin, Nottm Organ Society Dec 2021

Date viewed:

Gold and Silver Waltz, Nicholas Martin at Nottingham Organ Society Dec21

Date viewed:

Russ Conway tribute, Birthday Cakewalk, Nicholas Martin Technics Organ

Date viewed:

Tchaikovsky to Ragtime, Nicholas Martin, Organ piano voice, NOS Dec 21

Date viewed:

Jive/Rock 50s 60s, Nicholas Martin, Nottingham Organ Society Dec 21

Date viewed:

Warsaw Concerto, film Dangerous Moonlight, Nicholas Martin, Organ

Date viewed:

Wind Beneath my Wings, Nicholas Martin, Nottm Organ Society Dec 21

Date viewed:

Sleigh Ride, Merry little, Chestnuts roasting etc, Nicholas Martin 6 Dec21

Date viewed:

Blaze Away by Nicholas Martin at Nottingham Organ Society, 6 Dec 21

Date viewed:

Nicholas Martin, Technics G3 Organ, Opening selection, 6 December 21

Date viewed:

Nicholas and Maureen banter Nottingham Organ Society Concert 6 Dec21

Date viewed:

The Holy City, Jerusalem, Nicholas Martin, Nottingham Organ Society 6 Dec 21

Date viewed:

Chapter 23
Nottingham Organ Society – Year 2022

Brett Wales s performed the March 2022 Concert. Here are the titles loaded to YouTube

> Dualing Banjos, Brett Wales, Nottm Organ Society 2022

Date viewed:

> Mister Blue Sky, Brett Wales, Wersi Sonic Organ Mar 2022

Date viewed:

> Elvis tribute, Brett Wales, Can't Help Falling in Love, NOS Mar 22

Date viewed:

> A Love So Beautiful, Brett Wales, Nottm Organ Society March 22

Date viewed:

> The Sound of Silence, Brett Wales, Wersi Organ, March 2022

Date viewed:

Folsom Prison Blues, Brett Wales, Wersi, NOS March 2022

Date viewed:

Sabre Dance, Brett Wales, Nottm Organ Society March 2022

Date viewed:

In a Persian Market, Brett Wales, Nottm Organ Society March 2022

Date viewed:

Jimmy Smith Tribute, Brett Wales, Wersi, Nottm Organ Society, March 2022

Date viewed:

Queen Tribute, Brett Wales, Wersi, Nottm Organ Society March 2022

Date viewed:

Mozart, Rondo Alla Turca, Brett Wales, Wersi NOS March 2022

Date viewed:

Rock Medley, Brett Wales, Nottm Organ Society March 2022

Date viewed:

Lady in Red, Brett Wales, Wersi, Nottm Organ Society March 2022

Date viewed:

Big Band Swing, Brett Wales, Wersi, Nottm Organ Society, March 2022

Date viewed:

Romeo, Brett Wales, Wersi, Nottm Organ Society, March 2022

Date viewed:

Phantom of the Opera, Brett Wales, Wersi Sonic, NOS March 2022

Date viewed:

Pirates of the Caribbean, Brett Wales, Wersi, NOS March 2022

Date viewed:

Knowing Me, Knowing You, Brett Wales ,Wersi Sonic, NOS March 22

Date viewed:

Klaus Wunderlich Tribute, Brett Wales, NOS Mar 2022

Date viewed:

Oh My Beloved Father, Brett Wales, NOS March 2022

Date viewed:

Out of Africa, Brett Wales, Nottm Organ Society, March 2022

Date viewed:

And I Love You So, Brett Wales Wersi Sonic, NOS, March 2022

Date viewed:

Conquest of Paradise, Brett Wales, Wersi Sonic, NOS March 2022

Date viewed:

Brett Wales describes Multi Tracking and Klaus Wunderlich

Date viewed:

Michael Carter performed the May 2022 concert. Here are the titles loaded to YouTube

Romeo and Juliet theme, Nino Rota, Michael Carter, Yamaha Stagea, NOS

Date viewed:

Glass Mountain Legend, Michael Carter, Yamaha Stagea, Nottm OS

Date viewed:

Hoagy Carmichael, Tribute, Michael Carter, Yamaha Stagea, Nottm OS

Date viewed:

Meditation from Thais, Massenet, Michael Carter, Nottingham Organ Society

Date viewed:

War of the Worlds (End), Jeff Wayne, Michael Carter Nottm Organ Society

Date viewed:

Not a Day Goes By, Stephen Sondheim, Michael Carter, Nottm Organ Society

Date viewed:

Hammond Organ, Time is Tight/Green Onions, Michael Carter, Nottm OS

Date viewed:

Willy Wonka's Chocolate Factory, medley, Michael Carter, Nottm OS

Date viewed:

The Same Time Next Year, Michael Carter, Yamaha Stagea, Nottm OS

Date viewed:

It's a Sin (Pet Shop Boys), Michael Carter, Yamaha Organ, NOS

Date viewed:

Back to the Future. Film music, Michael Carter, Yamaha Organ, NOS

Date viewed:

Selection of 1957 tunes, Michael Carter, Yamaha Organ, Nottm OS

Date viewed:

Somewhere Out There, (An American Tale) Michael Carter, Yamaha, NOS

Date viewed:

Little Red Monkey, Michael Carter, Nottingham Organ Society May 2022

Date viewed:

Memories, Michael Carter, Yamaha Stagea, Nottm Organ Society

Date viewed:

Chorus Line selection, Michael Carter, Yamaha Organ, NOS

Date viewed:

A dream is a wish that your heart makes, Cinderella, Michael Carter, NOS

Date viewed:

Aces High, March, Ron Goodwin, Michael Carter, Nottm Organ Society

Date viewed:

Michael Carter, 'See you in my dreams' Nottingham Organ Society, May 2022

Date viewed:

Kevin Grunill performed the June 2022 concert. Here are titles loaded to YouTube

That's Entertainment, Kevin Grunill, Nottingham Organ Society June 2022

Date viewed:

As if we never said Goodbye, Sunset Boulevard, Kevin Grunill, NOS

Date viewed:

Waltz Medley, Kevin Grunill, Technics FN3 at Nottingham Organ Society

Date viewed:

Glen Miller Classics, Kevin Grunill at Nottingham Organ Society

Date viewed:

Show Tunes, Kevin Grunill at Nottingham Organ Society

Date viewed:

Big Band Medley, Kevin Grunill, Technics FN3 Organ, Nottm OS

Date viewed:

London by Night, Kevin Grunill, Nottingham Organ Society June 2022

Date viewed:

Great British Marches, Kevin Grunill, Technics Organ, Nottm Organ Society

Date viewed:

The Holy City, Kevin Grunill, Nottingham Organ Society, Technics FN3

Date viewed:

Wartime Nostalgic Selection, Kevin Grunill, Technics FA3 Organ, NOS

Date viewed:

Pomp & Circumstance 1, Kevin Grunill, Technics, Nottm Organ Society

Date viewed:

Brassed Off, March of the Cobblers, Kevin Grunill, Nottingham Organ Society

Date viewed:

Matthew Bason performed the August 2022 concert. These are titles loaded to YouTube. He brought along his Roland Atelier and Yamaha Keyboard. He used organ backing track and played his Weltmeister Accordion to provide a concert of varied entertainment.

Finale favourites, Matthew Bason at Nottingham Organ Society Aug 2022

Date viewed:

Radetzky March, Matthew Bason at Nottingham Organ Society

Date viewed:

Accordion, Liechtensteiner Polka, Matthew Bason at Nottingham Organ Society

Date viewed:

Pop hits across the decades, Matthew Bason, Nottm Organ Society

Date viewed:

Rock Medley from the 60's, Matthew Bason, Nottingham Organ Society

Date viewed:

Foot Tapper, (The Shadows hit) Matthew Bason at Nottm Organ Society

Date viewed:

Accordion Pennsylvania Polka, Matthew Bason, Nottm Organ Society

Date viewed:

Party Time, Mathew Bason, at Nottingham Organ Society Aug 2022

Date viewed:

Chariots of Fire, Mathew Bason Yamaha Keyboard, Nottm Organ Society

Date viewed:

Lion, Tiger, Cat medley, Yamaha Keyboard, Matthew Bason

Date viewed:

Accordion Blue Bell Polka, Matthew Bason, Nottm Organ Society

Date viewed:

Gabriel's Oboe, Roland Atelier, Matthew Bason, Nottm Organ Society

Date viewed:

Limehouse Blues, Trad Jazz played by Matthew Bason, Nottm Organ Society

Date viewed:

Circus Renze played by Matthew Bason, Nottingham Organ Society

Date viewed:

Chris Powell performed the November 2022 concert. Here are titles loaded to YouTube

Last Night of Proms, Chris Powell, Nottingham Organ Society Nov 2022

Date viewed:

Sing along selection, Chris Powell, Nottingham Organ Society

Date viewed:

Show Tunes, Chris Powell at Nottingham Organ Society 7 Nov 22

Date viewed:

Music for Dancing, Hammond Organ Sound, Chris Powell on Roland Atelier

Date viewed:

Dancing Queen & more Abba, Chris Powell, Nottingham Organ Society 7 Nov 22

Date viewed:

Great Escape March, Chris Powell, Nottingham Organ Society Nov 2022

Date viewed:

Wurlitzer Medley, Ballroom Tunes, Chris Powell, Nottingham Organ Society

Date viewed:

Morning in Cornwall, James Last, Chris Powell, Nottm Organ Society 7 Nov 22

Date viewed:

Sweet Caroline, Chris Powell, Nottingham Organ Society 7 Nov 22

Date viewed:

Beetles, Fab Four Tunes, Chris Powell, Nottingham Organ Society

Date viewed:

Orpheus in the Underworld with Can Can, Chris Powell, NOS

Date viewed:

Chris Barber & Kenny Ball Tribute by Chris Powell, NOS

Date viewed:

Elvis Presley Medley, Chris Powell, Nottingham Organ Society

Date viewed:

Happy Music, James Last, Chris Powell, Roland Atelier Organ Nov 22

Date viewed:

December 2022 featured another Nottm Organ Society Variety Show. Here are the titles loaded to YouTube

White Christmas with on screen words and final credits

Date viewed:

Santa Claus is coming to town, with on screen words

Date viewed:

Rudolph the Red nosed Reindeer with on screen words

Date viewed:

Hey Jude, Bonington Beatles, Arnold, Nottingham, (YouTubers can join in)

Date viewed:

Lady Madonna, Bonington Beatles, Arnold, Nottingham

Date viewed:

Musical Jigsaw composed and played by Mark Everatt, Nottm Organ Society

Date viewed:

Freddie Feelgood, QM Voice Quartet, Paul, Trevor, Adrain & Steve

Date viewed:

Love Me, (Elvis Presley) QM Voice Quartet, Paul, Trevor, Adrain & Steve

Date viewed:

To make you feel my love, Sung by the Major Oak Chorus

Date viewed:

Goodies & Get Up, danced by Shanade & Ciara, Adia Dance Studio, Nottm

Date viewed:

No Bad News, The Wiz, Danced by Azarah, Adia Dance Studio, Nottingham

Date viewed:

Get me bodied, Beyoncé, Danced by Naira, Adia Dance Studios. Nottingham

Date viewed:

Christmas Medley, Okey Dokey Voice Quartet, Bonington Theatre, Arnold, Nottm

Date viewed:

Sloop John B, Okey Dokey Voice Quartet, Pete, John, Shane & Mike

Date viewed:

Laughter in the Rain, Major Oak Chorus, Bonington Theatre, Arnold Nottm

Date viewed:

Java Jive, Major Oak Chorus, Bonington Theatre, Arnold, Nottingham

Date viewed:

While my guitar gently weeps, Bonington Beatles, 17 Dec 2022, Arnold, Nottm

Date viewed:

If I Fell in Love With You, Bonington Beatles, Arnold, Nottingham

Date viewed:

Get Back by Bonington Beatles, Nottingham Organ Society Arnold

Date viewed:

Mozart's Horn Concerto, Comedy Sketch devised and performed by Keith Harding}

Date viewed:

Chapter 24
Nottingham Organ Society – Year 2023

Brett Wales performed the January 2023 concert. Here are titles loaded to YouTube

    Falling in Love With You, Brett Wales, Wersi Sonic, Nottm Organ Society

Date viewed:

    Will you Love Me Tomorrow, Brett Wales, Wersi Sonic, Organ

Date viewed:

    Blanket on the Ground, Brett Wales, Wersi Sonic, Nottm Organ Society

Date viewed:

    How deep is your Love, Brett Wales with the Bee Gees, Wersi Sonic Organ

Date viewed:

Human voices inserted in Wersi Sonic, Brett Wales demonstrates with Bee Gees

Date viewed:

St Louis Blues, Brett Wales, Wersi Sonic, Nottingham Organ Society

Date viewed:

Super Trooper, Brett Wales, Wersi Sonic, Nottingham Organ Society

Date viewed:

Robert Davies performed the February 2023 concert. Here are titles loaded to YouTube

Phantom of the opera selection, Robert Davies, Nottingham Organ Society

Date viewed:

Rouge ou noir, played by Robert Davies, Nottingham Organ Society

Date viewed:

Larien da Saba played by Robert Davies at Nottingham Organ Society

Date viewed:

Unforgettable, arr Nelson Riddle, played by Robert Davies Organ

Date viewed:

You don't have to say you love me, Dusty Springfield, Robert Davies Organ

Date viewed:

Elizabethan Serenade, Ronald Binge played by Robert Davies Organ

Date viewed:

Funiculi Funicular, Helmet Lotte version, Robert Davies, NOS

Date viewed:

When You Tell Me That You Love Me (Diane Ross), Robert Davies Organ

Date viewed:

Plink, Plank, Plunk Leroy Anderson played by Robert Davies, Organ

Date viewed:

I Need To Be In Love (Carpenters) played by Robert Davies, organ

Date viewed:

Toccata & Fugue played by Robert Davies organ, apologies to J S Bach

Date viewed:

Sports Report signature tune, Out Of The Blue, Played by Robert Davies, organ

Date viewed:

Pavane, Gabriel Fauré played by Robert Davies, Nottingham Organ Society

Date viewed:

It had better be tonight, Henry Mancini played by Robert Davies Organ

Date viewed:

If I never sing another song' played by Robert Davies, Organ

Date viewed:

Childhood, (Michael Jackson), Robert Davies, Nottm Organ Society

Date viewed:

Klaus Wunderlich's Amore Grande, Robert Davies, Nottm Organ Society

Date viewed:

The Moldau, Smetana, Robert Davies, Nottm Organ Society Feb 2023

Date viewed:

James Bond, 3 tunes, Robert Davies, Nottingham Organ Society

Date viewed:

The Hungry Years by Neil Sedaka, Robert Davies, Nottm Organ Society

Date viewed:

March of the Cobblers, Brassed off, Robert Davies Nottm Organ Society

Date viewed:

You're my World, Robert Davies, Organ, (Cilla Black) Nottm Organ Society

Date viewed:

Shadows medley, Robert Davies, Nottingham Organ Society Feb 2023

Date viewed:

Saving all my love for you Robert Davies, Nottingham Organ Society

Date viewed:

There's no business like show business, Robert Davies, Nottm Organ Society

Date viewed:

The War of the Worlds, Robert Davies, Nottingham Organ Society

Date viewed:

Nicholas Martin performed the March 2023 concert. Here are the titles loaded to YouTube

Warsaw Concerto, Dangerous Moonlight, Nickolas Martin Nottm Organ Society

Date viewed:

Goodbye with 12 Street Rag, Nicholas Martin, Nottingham Organ Society

Date viewed:

Side Saddle, Russ Conway Tribute by Nicholas Martin, Nottm Organ Society

Date viewed:

Windows of Paris to Manhattan, Nicholas Martin Nottm Organ Society

Date viewed:

Intermezzo, Cavalleria Rusticana, Mascagni, Nicholas Martin, Nottm Organ Society

Date viewed:

Les Toreadors from Carmen, Bizet, Nicholas Martin, Nottm Organ Society

Date viewed:

The Mission Theme by Ennio Morricone, Nicholas Martin, Nottm Organ Society

Date viewed:

1960s Medley, Nicholas Martin at Nottingham Organ Society

Date viewed:

Dambusters, Eric Coates, Nicholas Martin, Nottingham Organ Society

Date viewed:

Old Pi-Anna Rag, Cabaret, 42nd Street Nicholas Martin, Nottm Organ Society

Date viewed:

Show Tunes, Joseph, Sound of Music, Les Miserable, Nicholas Martin Organ
Date viewed:

Waltz from Masquerade suite, Khachaturian, Nicholas Martin Organ NOS
Date viewed:

Summer place, The Entertainer, A Bridge too far, Nicholas Martin Organ NOS
Date viewed:

Legend of the Glass Mountain, Nicholas Martin, Nottingham Organ Society
Date viewed:

Lend me your Ear, Marching & Waltzing Nicholas Martin, Nottm Organ Society
Date viewed:

You'll Never Walk Alone from Carousel, Nicholas Martin, Nottm Organ Society
Date viewed:

Autism, Nicholas Martin BEM, organist describes, Miracles to Believe In, NOS
Date viewed:

Eric Shaw was one of the original performers at Nottingham Organ Society and was the resident organist at Nottingham Ice Stadium for many years, He played music for dancing at the Calverton Minors Welfare where Joan and I danced to his music for about five years. These videos are taken from two audio tapes originally produced by Eric which I bought from him in 1984. I have used a picture taken at the Original Nottingham Ice Stadium for the second tape. Eric Shaw passed away in the summer of 2024. My tribute to him is the music that he played being available on YouTube.

Here are titles loaded to YouTube in 2023

Strict Tempo Dance Music by Eric Shaw – Quickstep

Date viewed:

Strict Tempo Dance Music by Eric Shaw – Pride of Erin Waltz

Date viewed:

Strict Tempo Dance Music by Eric Shaw – Rhumba

Date viewed:

Strict Tempo Dance Music by Eric Shaw – Sequence Waltz

Date viewed:

Strict Tempo Dance Music by Eric Shaw – Saunter

Date viewed:

Strict Tempo Dance Music by Eric Shaw – Sequence Cha Cha

Date viewed:

Strict Tempo Dance Music by Eric Shaw – Slow Foxtrot

Date viewed:

Strict Tempo Dance Music by Eric Shaw – Melody or Sequence Foxtrot
Date viewed:

Strict Tempo Dance Music by Eric Shaw – Bossa Nova
Date viewed:

Strict Tempo Dance Music by Eric Shaw – Mayfair Quickstep
Date viewed:

Strict Tempo Dance Music by Eric Shaw – Cuban Swing or Rhumba
Date viewed:

Strict Tempo Dance Music by Eric Shaw – Square or Sequence Tango
Date viewed:

Strict Tempo Dance Music by Eric Shaw – The Maxina
Date viewed:

I'll see you in my dreams. Eric Shaw organ 1984. With on screen words
Date viewed:

I'll be seeing you, organ, Eric Shaw 1984 with on screen words
Date viewed:

Sweet Georgia Brown, Eric Shaw organ 1984 with on screen words

Date viewed:

The shadow of your smile, Eric Shaw organ 1984 with on screen words

Date viewed:

Cavatina, Eric Shaw organ 1984 with on screen words

Date viewed:

Bless you for being an Angel, organ Eric Shaw 1984 with on screen words

Date viewed:

I want to be happy, Eric Shaw organ 1984 with on screen words

Date viewed:

Blue Spanish Eyes, Eric Shaw organ 1984 with on screen words

Date viewed:

Amazing Grace, Eric Shaw organ 1984, with on screen words

Date viewed:

Fly me to the moon, Eric Shaw organ 1984 with on screen words

Date viewed:

Tea for two, Eric Shaw Organ 1984, With on screen words

Date viewed:

Till (the moon deserts the sky), Eric Shaw organ 1984 with on screen words

Date viewed:

Calcutta (the Ladies of) Eric Shaw organ 1984 with on screen words

Date viewed:

Isle of Capri, Eric Shaw organ 1984 with on screen words

Date viewed:

All of me, Eric Shaw organ 1984 with on screen words

Date viewed:

September in the Rain, Eric Shaw organ 1984 with on screen words

Date viewed:

Moonlight serenade, Eric Shaw organ with on screen words

Date viewed:

Toy Balloons, Eric Shaw organ 1984 with on screen words

Date viewed:

San Fransisco, Eric Shaw organ 1984 with on screen words

Date viewed:

Love story, Eric Shaw organ 1984 with on screen words

Date viewed:

So nice, Eric Shaw organ 1984 on screen words

Date viewed:

It had to be you, Eric Shaw organ 1984 with on screen words

Date viewed:

Mistakes, Eric Shaw organ 1984 with some on screen words – see description

Date viewed:

Perfidia, Eric Shaw organ 1984 with on screen words

Date viewed:

Green Eyes, Eric Shaw organ 1984 with on screen words

Date viewed:

S'wonderful, Eric Shaw organ 1984 with on screen words

Date viewed:

Aqua Marina, played by Eric Shaw organ, 1984 with on screen words

Date viewed:

Tribute to Hammond Organist Eric Shaw, introduction to videos loaded

Date viewed:

Matthew Bason performed the April 2023 concert with Roland Atelier organ and Yamaha Keyboard. He also played his Weltmeister Accordion. Here are the titles loaded to YouTube

Radetzky March, Matthew Bason, Nottingham Organ Society April 2023

Date viewed:

Zorba's Dance, Matthew Bason, Nottingham Organ Society

Date viewed:

Dancing Mood, Over the years, Matthew Bason, Nottm Organ Society

Date viewed:

Comedians and Toreadors, Mathew Bason, Nottingham Organ Society

Date viewed:

Opera Medley, Matthew Bason, Roland Atelier, Nottm Organ Society

Date viewed:

Accordion, Scottish Medley, Matthew Bason, Nottingham Organ Society

Date viewed:

Accordion, Bridges of Paris, Matthew Bason, Nottm Organ Society

Date viewed:

Country Music Medley, Matthew Bason, Nottingham Organ Society

Date viewed:

Piano Greats medley. ending with a sing along, Matthew Bason, Organ

Date viewed:

When Your'e Smiling, Bye bye Blackbird, Matthew Bason, organ & Vocals

Date viewed:

Night & Day S'wonderful, Customer Services, Matthew Bason, Organ

Date viewed:

Gabriel's Oboe, The Mission, Matthew Bason Nottingham Organ Society

Date viewed:

50's & 60's pop favourites, Matthew Bason, Nottingham Organ Society

Date viewed:

Samba Set, Matthew Bason, Nottm Organ Society April 2023

Date viewed:

Robert Davies performed the August 2023 concert. Here are titles loaded to YouTube

Discotime/Summertime, Robert Davies arr Klaus Wunderlich at NOS

Date viewed:

Now, played by Robert Davies on Yamaha Genos, Bonington Theatre, NOS

Date viewed:

One Night Only, Robert Davies, Nottm Organ Society Aug 2023

Date viewed:

That's What Friends Are For, Robert Davies, Nottm Organ Society

Date viewed:

Spitfire Prelude, William Walton, Robert Davies, Nottm Organ Society

Date viewed:

Sportpalast Waltz, Robert Davies, Nottm Organ Society

Date viewed:

Moonlight Serenade, Robert Davies, Bonington Theatre Arnold Nottm

Date viewed:

Woman in Love, Robert Davies on Yamaha Genos, NOS Aug 2023

Date viewed:

The Moldau, Smetana, Robert Davies, Yamaha Genos, Bonington NOS

Date viewed:

Pie Jesu, Robert Davies, Yamaha Genos, Nottm Organ Society

Date viewed:

Got the World on a String, Robert Davies, Nottm Organ Society

Date viewed:

Caruso, Robert Davies, Yamaha Genos, Nottm Organ Society

Date viewed:

New York, New York, Robert Davies, Yamaha Genos, Nottm Organ Society

Date viewed:

Belle of the Ball by Leroy Anderson, Robert Davies, Yamaha Genos

Date viewed:

Mark Everatt and others performed the September 2023 concert. Here are titles put on YouTube

Where Man Goes, Mark Everatt, NG42, Nottm Organ Society Sep 2023

Date viewed:

Six Degrees of Separation, NG42 Trio, Nottm Organ Society Sep 2023

Date viewed:

Always Look on the Bright Side of Life, Oakie Dokie singers, Sep 2023

Date viewed:

Java Jive. Okie Dokie singers, Bonington Theatre, Arnold, Nottm Sep 2023

Date viewed:

Pink Panther Theme, Mark Everatt. Bonington Theatre Arnold Nottm Sep 2023

Date viewed:

What a Wonderful World, Mark Everatt, Yamaha Genos. Nottingham 2023

Date viewed:

Baby Elephant Walk, Mark Everatt Yamaha Genos, Bonington Theatre Nottm

Date viewed:

Mornings at Seven, Mark Everatt, Yamaha Genos, Bonington Theatre, Arnold Nottm

Date viewed:

Somewhere Over the Rainbow, Okie Dokie Singers, Nottingham

Date viewed:

Wheels Cha Cha, Mark Everatt, Bonington Theatre Arnold Nottm Sep 23

Date viewed:

My Love, Mark Everatt, Genos, Bonington Theatre, Arnold Nottingham 2023

Date viewed:

Top of the World, Mark Everatt, Yamaha Genos, Bonington Theatre Nottm 2023

Date viewed:

Swinging Safari, Mark Everatt, Yamaha Genos Bonington Theatre, Nottm 2023

Date viewed:

Telstar, Yamaha Genos, arranged/played by Mark Everatt Nottingham 2023

Date viewed:

Two by Two, NG42 Trio, Bonington Theatre, Arnold Nottingham 2023

Date viewed:

A Film Called Deja Vu, NG42 Trio, Bonington Theatre, Arnold Nottm 2023

Date viewed:

One Day at a Time, NG42 Trio, Bonington Theatre, Arnold Nottingham 2023

Date viewed:

For the Longest Time, Okie Dokie Singers, Bonington Theatre, Arnold 2023

Date viewed:

Can You Feel the Love Tonight, Okie Dokie Singers, Arnold Nottm Sep 2023

Date viewed:

Kiss me Me Honey Honey, Kiss Me, Mark Everatt Yamaha Genos, 2023

Date viewed:

Albatross, Mark Everatt, Yamaha Genos, Bonington Theatre, Nottm 2023

Date viewed:

Have I the Right, Mark Everatt, Yamaha Genos, Bonington Theatre 2023

Date viewed:

Something, Okie Dokie Singers, Bonington Theatre Arnold Nottm 2023

Date viewed:

Love Me, Oakie Dokie Singers, Bonington Theatre, Arnold Nottm 2023

Date viewed:

He Ain't Heavy He's My Brother, Mark Everatt, Yamaha Genos, 2023

Date viewed:

So Whats New, Herb Alpert, Mark Everatt, Yamaha Genos Nottm 2023

Date viewed:

Music Box Dancer, Mark Everatt, Yamaha Genos, Bonington, Arnold 2023

Date viewed:

James Bond Theme, Mark Everatt, Genos organ, Arnold, Nottingham 2023

Date viewed:

Chris and Joanne Powell performed the November 2023 concert. Here are titles loaded to YouTube

Duelling Banjos, Chris and Joanne Powell, Nottingham Organ Society Nov 2023

Date viewed:

Wartime music, Chris & Joanne Powell, Nottingham Organ Society Nov 2023

Date viewed:

Show tunes, Chris & Joanne Powell, Nottm Organ Society Nov 2023

Date viewed:

Country songs, Chris and Joanne Powell, Nottm Organ Society Nov 2023

Date viewed:

Rocking & Rolling, Chris & Joanne Powell, Nottingham Organ Society Nov 2023

Date viewed:

Wonderful world/Falling in love, Chris & Joanne Powell Nottm OS Nov 23

Date viewed:

March 'Help yourself' Chris & Joanne Powell, Nottingham Organ Society, Nov 2023

Date viewed:

Latin American medley, Chris & Joanne Powell, Nottm Organ Society Nov 2023

Date viewed:

How Great Thou Art, Chris & Joanne Powell at Nottingham Organ Society Nov 2023

Date viewed:

Toccata JS Bach played by Chris Powell, Nottm Organ Society Nov 2023

Date viewed:

Nuns Chorus, Casanova, Chris & Joanne Powell, Nottm Organ Society Nov 2023

Date viewed:

Scottish Medley, Chris & Joanne Powell, Nottm Organ Society, Nov 2023

Date viewed:

Hungarian Dance, Chris & Joanne Powell, Nottm Organ Society Nov 2023

Date viewed:

Wedding & Love Songs, Chris & Joanne Powell, Nottm Organ Society, Nov 2023

Date viewed:

Happy Music, (James Last) Chris & Joanne Powell, Nottm Organ Society Nov 2023

Date viewed:

In December 2023 I put together a video of not stop music from various performers and loaded it to You Tube with this title.

Organ & Keyboards 1 hour of uninterrupted music from Nottm Organ Society

Date viewed:

This is the description that I used. 'This is a gift to people who like music played on organs and keyboards. The performers are Nicholas Martin, Robert Davies, Brett Wales Chris & Joanne Powell and Matthew Bason. I have selected music from Nottingham Organ Society Concerts at the Bonington Theatre, Arnold Nottingham. Michael Parkinson'

Chapter 25
Nottingham Organ Society – Year 2024

Robert Davies performed the 5 February 2024 concert. Here are titles loaded to YouTube.

Belle of the Ball, Leroy Anderson. Robert Davies, Yamaha Genos Organ 5 Feb 24

Date viewed:

Saving all my love for you, Robert Davies, Yamaha Genos Organ 5 Feb 24

Date viewed:

Apache & Dance On, Robert Davies Yamaha Genos, NOS 5 Feb 24

Date viewed:

New York, New York, Robert Davies, Yamaha Genos, NOS 5 Feb 24

Date viewed:

Your My World, Robert Davies, Yamaha Genos, Nottingham Organ Society 5 Feb 24

Date viewed:

Caruso played by Robert Davies, Yamaha Genos Organ, NOS 5 Feb 24

Date viewed:

Night and Day played by Robert Davies, Yamaha Genos Organ on 5 Feb 24

Date viewed:

He ain't heavy he's my brother, Robert Davies, NOS 5 Feb 24

Date viewed:

Calon Lân Welch Hymn, Robert Davies, Yamaha Genos, NOS 5 Feb 24

Date viewed:

Eye of the Tiger, Robert Davies, Yamaha Genos, NOS 5 Feb 24

Date viewed:

Love Story played by Robert Davies on Yamaha Genos, NOS 5 Feb 24

Date viewed:

Woman in Love, Robert Davies, Yamaha Genos, NOS 5 Feb 24

Date viewed:

It had better be tonight, Robert Davies, Yamaha Genos, NOS 5 Feb 24

Date viewed:

Pavanne, Gabriel Fauré on Yamaha Genos by Robert Davies NOS 5 Feb 24

Date viewed:

Sportpalast Waltzer played by Robert Davies on Yamaha Genos, NOS 5 Feb 24

Date viewed:

Childhood, written by Michael Jackson, Robert Davies, Yamaha Genos Feb 2024

Date viewed:

Moonlight Serenade, Robert Davies on Yamaha Genos, NOS 5 Feb 24

Date viewed:

Ordinary Fool played by Robert Davies, Yamaha Genos, NOS 5 Feb 2024

Date viewed:

Funiculi Funicular played by Robert Davies, Yamaha Genos at NOS on 5 Feb 24

Date viewed:

Plink plank plunk, Robert Davies on Yamaha Genos at NOS 5 Feb 24

Date viewed:

Elizabethan Serenade, Robert Davies, Yamaha Genos at NOS 5 Feb 2024

Date viewed:

Unforgettable, Robert Davies playing Yamaha Genos Organ at NOS on 5 Feb 2024

Date viewed:

Calling All Workers, Robert Davies at Nottingham Organ Society 5 Feb 2024

Date viewed:

That's what friends are for, Robert Davies, Yamaha Genos at NOS 5 Feb 2024

Date viewed:

I can't give you anything (but my love) & The Hustle, Robert Davies NOS Feb 2024

Date viewed:

Rouge ou Noir, Robert Davies, Yamaha Genos at NOS on 5 Feb 2024

Date viewed:

La Reine De Sarba, Robert Davies, Yamaha Genos Organ, NOS 5 Feb 24

Date viewed:

Summertime, Robert Davies, Yamaha Genos, NOS 5 Feb 24

Date viewed:

Brett Wales performed the March 2024 concert. Here are titles loaded to YouTube.

Jerusalema, Brett Wales, Wersi Sonic, Nottingham Organ Society March 2024

Date viewed:

Take on me, Brett Wales, Wersi Sonic, Nottingham Organ Society March 2024

Date viewed:

Oh my beloved Father, Brett Wales, Wersi, Nottm Organ Society March 2024

Date viewed:

Tico Tico, Brett Wales, Wersi Sonic, Nottm Organ Society March 2024

Date viewed:

Land down under, Brett Wales, Wersi, Nottm Organ Society March 2024

Date viewed:

La vie en rose, Brett Wales, Wersi, Nottingham Organ Society, March 2024

Date viewed:

Green Onions, Brett Wales, Wersi Sonic, Nottm Organ Society March 2024

Date viewed:

Dance of the little Swans, Brett Wales, Wersi, Nottm Organ Society Mar 2024

Date viewed:

Give me the night, Brett Wales, Wersi, Nottm Organ Society, March 2024

Date viewed:

Phantom of the Opera, Brett Wales, Nottm Organ Society March 2024,

Date viewed:

Flying Home, Brett Wales, Wersi Sonic, Nottm Organ Society March 2024

Date viewed:

Romeo, Brett Wales, Wersi Sonic, Nottingham Organ Society March 2024

Date viewed:

Go your own way, Brett Wales, Nottingham Organ Society Mar 2024,

Date viewed:

When someone thinks you're wonderful. Brett Wales, NOS Mar 24,,

Date viewed:

William Tell, Brett Wales, Wersi Sonic, Nottm Organ Society March 2024

Date viewed:

This guys in love with you, Brett Wales, Nottm Organ Society Mar 24,

Date viewed:

Ronda a la Turk, Brett Wales, Wersi, Nottm Organ Society Mar 2024

Date viewed:

Freddie Mercury/Queen, Brett Wales, Nottm Organ Society March 2024,

Date viewed:

Nights in White Satin, Brett Wales, Nottm Organ Society, March 2024

Date viewed:

Bumble Bee Rock, Brett Wales, Wersi Sonic, Nottm Organ Society March 2024

Date viewed:

Just pretend, Brett Wales, Nottingham Organ Society March 2024,

Date viewed:

MacArthur Park, Brett Wales, Wersi, Nottm Organ Society March 2024

Date viewed:

Folsom Prison Blues, Brett Wales, Wersi, Nottm Organ Society March 24,

Date viewed:

Jon Smith performed at the Bonington Theatre on 6 May 2024 but created the most difficult situation I have encountered as videographer for Nottingham Organ Society. I had attended concerts performed by Jon with Chiho Sunamoto but for various reasons have never videoed them. Then, in November 2018, I learned the devastating news that Chiho had died.

The next occasion that Jon played for NOS after her death was in January 2022 and he gave permission for me to video the whole concert. Half way through the first half Jon spoke a tribute to Chiho and played a sound recording of her playing. It was described by Michael Carpenter in the February edition of 'Harmony' as 'The Late Lamented Chiho Sunamoto now made an invisible guest appearance as Jon ran a recording of Send in the Clowns in a beautiful arrangement for piano, flute and voices on the Genos'. There was not a dry eye in the Theatre and I noticed that Jon was visibly emotional as well. At the end of the performance Jon asked me not to load anything to YouTube, he said, 'I was in pieces'. Both he and I knew why without need for discussion.

When Jon performed again for NOS on 6 May 2024 he again gave permission for me to record the whole of the concert. I realised that he was experiencing great difficulty in setting up the voices and settings for the individual pieces but that was no problem to me because I edit my YouTube loadings to start at the first note played and finish before the audience applause. We spoke at the interval and Jon told me that he was suffering from Long Covid and a degenerative lung condition. He also apologised for his performance which he said was below his usual standard. I told him that he was too self deprecating and I thought his playing was brilliant. At the end of the concert Jon told me that he wanted to watch and listen to everything he had performed before giving permission for YouTube. I reluctantly agreed and used a system of loading as Unlisted and sending Jon the links so that he could decide what could be made Public.

The following weeks and months involved many telephone conversations but no decision. After nine weeks I asked Jon if he could send me any DVD recording of he and Chiho playing together. He readily agreed and commented 'That will be better than me playing on my own'. However, another three weeks went by and nothing had arrived so I decided to give up and not include this story in my book or to load anything to YouTube. As if by magic, later that morning, the promised DVD from Jon dropped through my letter box. The date was 2 August 2024, about 12 weeks after Jon had performed the May 2024 concert for Nottingham Organ Society.

When I watched the DVD of Jon and Chiho I realised why he did not want his solo performances to be loaded to YouTube, they were much better together. He and Chiho had been living together since 2005 but sometime before their marriage on 18 March 2017 Chiho had been diagnosed with inoperable cancer so their performance together at the Crossing Church & Centre, Worksop in 2018 was very special to them. I spoke again to Jon by telephone because I was concerned about copyright of the DVD but Jon assured me that I could load any or all of the DVD to YouTube. He also gave permission for me to load just his encore of his solo Nottingham concert but no more. The DVD that Jon sent to me had been videoed from the back of the Hall with the backs of people sitting in the front rows in vision. I used a technique that I have devised to video parts of the screen. The vision is slightly impaired but the sound is good. The YouTube title of the encore at Nottingham is

I Won't Send Roses:Show business Jon Smith, 3 Cheers at NOS (I am sure that this song was a Tribute to Chiho)

Date viewed:

The 22 YouTube titles from the Chiho and Jon concert are listed as follows.
(Because of the background story, I think 'Love me Tender' is the most emotional and poignant of the whole concert).

Classical theme & Stardust, Jon Smith piano, Chiho Sunamoto, organ

Date viewed:

Beauty and the Beast played by Chiho Sunamoto on Yamaha organ

Date viewed:

Star Wars Tune, Chiho Sunamoto playing Yamaha organ 2017

Date viewed:

I've Got You Under My Skin, Chiho Sunamoto Yamaha organ, Jon Smith Vocal

Date viewed:

Love Me Tender. An emotional wedding song by Chiho Sunamoto and Jon Smith

Date viewed:

What a Wonderful World Jon Smith, Hohner Melodica, Chiho Sunamoto Yamaha organ

Date viewed:

Stranger in Paradise, Chiho Sunamoto organ, Jon Smith piano – Composed by Borodin

Date viewed:

Tea For Two, Jon Smith piano, Chiho Sunamoto organ, Worksop, Nottinghamshire 2017

Date viewed:

Heavenly Light, Chiho Sunamoto Yamaha organ, at The Crossings Church & Centre

Date viewed:

Battle Hymn of the Republic, Jon Smith piano Chiho Sunamoto Yamaha organ

Date viewed:

It Don't mean a thing If it ain't got that swing Chiho Sunamoto & Jon Smith

Date viewed:

Moonlight Serenade, Chiho Sunamoto Yamaha Organ

Date viewed:

Rhapsody on a Theme of Paganini, Chiho Sunamoto, Yamaha organ

Date viewed:

Pictures at an Exhibition, Chiho Sunamoto, Yamaha organ

Date viewed:

Theme from The Godfather Chiho Sunamoto, Yamaha organ

Date viewed:

Misty Chiho Sunamoto, Yamaha Organ, Jon Smith playing Hohner Melodica

Date viewed:

Carmen excerpts played by Chiho Sunamoto on Makin Westmoreland Organ

Date viewed:

You Make Me Feel So Young, Chiho Sunamoto – Yamaha organ Jon Smith vocals

Date viewed:

Bewitched Bothered and Bewildered , Chiho Sunamoto & Jon Smith

Date viewed:

I've Got Rhythm, Chiho Sunamoto and Jon Smith

Date viewed:

Pomp & Circumstance No 1 Chiho Sunamoto & Jon Smith – organs

Date viewed:

That's All, Chiho Sunamoto & Jon Smith at Worksop

Date viewed:

I acknowledge the work done by Phillip Howarth, Peter Warren and Brian Howarth of Woodside Productions for the original DVD. Chiho Sunamoto and Jon Smith 'East Meets West' Live in concert at The Crossings Church & Centre, Worksop which I used to create these videos.
– Michael Parkinson

Nicholas Martin performed the July 2024 concert playing his Technics GA3. Here are the titles of videos loaded to YouTube

Hey look me over, Face the Music, Putting on the Ritz, You do something to Me, Nicholas Martin NOS

Date viewed:

Highland Cathedral, Amazing Grace & Leicester Square Rag Nicholas Martin, NOS July 2024

Date viewed:

Angel in Blue played by Nicholas Martin on Technics organ, Nottm Organ Society

Date viewed:

Gold and Silver Waltz, Franz Lehar, Nicholas Martin at Nottingham Organ Society

Date viewed:

Great Little Army, Old Comrades, Blaze Away, Nicholas Martin, Technics Organ at NOS

Date viewed:

Cavalleria Rusticana, Intermezzo composed by Pietro Mascagni, Played by Nicholas Martin, Organ

Date viewed:

Meditation from Thais composed by Jules Massenet played by Nicholas Martin on Technics organ

Date viewed:

Sweet Caroline, Unchained Melody, Side Saddle, Bobbys Girl, Walking back to Happiness NOS

Date viewed:

Forgotten Dreams, All the Way, 12 Street Rag Nicholas Martin Nottm Organ Society 8 Jul 2024

Date viewed:

Dizzy Fingers, Misty, Lola Piano Style, Nicholas Martin on Technics Organ at NOS

Date viewed:

Lullaby of Birdland, Ain't Misbehaving, Sophisticated Lady, Black & White Rag, Nicholas Martin

Date viewed:

The Second Waltz Shostakovich Nicholas Martin, Nottm Organ Society 8 July 24

Date viewed:

Emerdale Farm, Last of Summer Wine, Match of the Day themes Nicholas Martin

Date viewed:

Fields of Gold, Love Many Splendored Thing & Latin Medley Nicholas Martin

Date viewed:

A Nightingale Sang in Berkeley Square & Nostalgic Songs, Nicholas Martin

Date viewed:

Can't help falling in Love, Nicholas Martin at Nottm Organ Society

Date viewed:

Claire Greig performed the concert at Nottingham Organ Society on 5 August 2024

Here are the titles of videos loaded to YouTube

Beer Barrel Polka, Rosamunde, Roll out the Barrel, Claire Greig, Wersi organ

Date viewed:

Happy Music by James Last, Claire Greig at Nottm Organ Society, Aug 2024

Date viewed:

Claire Greig technical talk about the Wersi OAX1 Duo Organ. Just for organ enthusiasts

Date viewed:

Morning, written by Edvard Grieg played by Claire Greig on Wersi Organ at Nottingham Organ Society

Date viewed:

Ballade Pour Adeline, Claire Greig, Wersi organ, Bonington Theatre for Nottm OS

Date viewed:

Gold Spandau Ballet Claire Greig, Wersi organ at Nottingham Organ Society Aug 2024

Date viewed:

Save the best till last, Claire Greig, Wersi organ, Nottingham Organ Society 5 Aug 24

Date viewed:

The Godfather, Film Theme, Claire Greig at Nottingham Organ Society on 5 Aug 24

Date viewed:

Typewriter (Leroy Anderson), played by Claire Greig on Wersi organ at NOS

Date viewed:

Morning in Cornwall by James Last, Claire Greig playing Wersi organ at NOS

Date viewed:

Clarinet & Tritsch Tratsch Polka, Claire Greig, Nottm Organ Society 5 Aug 24

Date viewed:

Elizabethan Serenade, Claire Greig at Nottingham Organ Society on 5 Aug 2024

Date viewed:

Toccata by Wider, Claire Greig playing Wersi organ at Nottm OS

Date viewed:

Out of Africa, Claire Greig at Nottingham Organ Society on 5 Aug 2024

Date viewed:

St Elmo's Fire theme , Claire Greig Wersi Organ at Nottingham Organ Society Aug 2024

Date viewed:

Circus Renz, Claire Greig, Bonington Theatre Arnold, Nottingham Organ Society Aug 2024

Date viewed:

Rock Me played by Claire Greig on Wersi at Nottingham Organ Society on 5 Aug 2024

Date viewed:

Semper Fedelis, Stars & Stripes, Washington Post, Claire Greig, Wersi organ at NOS

Date viewed:

Forest Gump, Feather Theme, Claire Greig, Wersi Organ, Nottingham Organ Society Aug 2024

Date viewed:

Winter Games, Olympic TV theme , Claire Greig, Wersi organ at NOS 5 Aug 2024

Date viewed:

Voices of Spring & Roses From the South, Waltzing with Claire Greig, Wersi Organ

Date viewed:

Goodbye to Love, Claire Greig on Wersi at Nottingham Organ Society

Date viewed:

Chariots of Fire, Claire Greig playing the theme on Wersi Organ at NOS

Date viewed:

Handbags & Glad Rags, Claire Greig at Nottingham Organ Society Aug 2024

Date viewed:

ET Film Theme, Claire Greig at Nottm Organ Society

Date viewed:

Dreaming Ballerina, Claire Greig playing Wersi organ at NOS

Date viewed:

Orpheus in the Underworld, Claire Grieg, Wersi Organ at Nottingham OS

Date viewed:

Second Waltz, Dmitri Shostakovich, Claire Grieg, Wersi organ at NOS

Date viewed:

Chapter 26
Nottingham Organ Society – The first 30 years 1967/97
by Michael Carpenter

In the 1960s, the Hammond Organ was the market leader by many a mile, though competition was beginning to increase. In a desire to give its customers a little extra and so perhaps consolidate customer loyalty, Hammond Organ (UK) Ltd set up a series of owners' clubs. They did this through their network of official dealers, it was named 'The Hammond Organ Societies'. Before long there were lots of them, but not in Nottingham. The problem here was that there were two official dealers: Cranes on Derby Road and Farmers (Pearsons) on Long Row. Exploratory talks were held with the Hammond company but it was decided that nothing could be done under the circumstances. Later on, Cranes closed down so Mike Slater and Phylis Smedley got together with Farmers to approach Hammonds again. This time the way was clear.

With the aid of Farmers' mailing list, Mike arranged two concerts at the Grey Goose in Gedling (of which he was resident organist) under the auspices of the Cinema Organ Society (of which he was an officer). These went so well that it was decided to call a meeting at the Grey Goose on 18th October 1967 and here the Nottingham Hammond Organ Society was founded. Mike Slater became Secretary and Jim Lambert represented the dealer.

Monthly Recitals commenced in November at the Grey Goose using Mike's organ and the first edition of the *Newsletter* was published in December. Informal meetings, held in Pearsons' Staff Dining Room began in February 1968.

Fairly soon, all meetings were transferred to the Trent Room in the basement of the Odeon Cinema. This was at the time an ideal venue, attractive, central, easily accessible from all parts by public transport and had on street parking. It was just across the road from Pearsons so could be furnished with organs at no cost. In the early days, the Hammond Company issued a magazine to societies with the title of *Harmony*. The discontinuation of that magazine at the end of 1968 would later open a door for us.

Due to a further remodelling of the Odeon, the Trent Room closed and we had to leave, our last meeting there being in April 1969. Informal meetings moved back to Pearsons and Recitals to the Polish Club, off Sherwood Rise. In July 1969, Mike Slater turned the *Newsletter* from a 'letter headed' sheet to a 'booklet' form and sought suggestions for a name. The end of our second year saw some significant developments. In October 1969 our first President, Denis Matthews, was installed by Keith Beckingham of Hammond Organ (UK) Ltd. At the Annual General Meeting in November it was announced that Pearsons were to impose a hire charge for organs taken outside their own premises and that, to counter this, the Society would buy its own organ. In December our magazine got its name – *Harmony* – with the permission of Hammonds, and was made self supporting through advertising.

Our organ, a C-3 with two PR-40s tone cabinets, made its debut at the January 1970 recital. There was applause and 'oohs' and 'aahs' as the stage curtains opened to reveal its brilliant white console, still exuding the smell of fresh cellulose paint. In all honesty that organ did cause us problems. Subscriptions had to go up (agreed at the AGM) though they would have had to anyway to cover the hire charge, loans had to be sought from members and intense fund raising (not always successful) had to be undertaken. The supplier was finally paid off in December 1971 and members loans in April 1972. The organ had had a hard working life in a club and needed an overhaul soon after purchase, while maintenance, storage, transport and handling were problems that were to haunt the Society organs ever after. Once the knack of successful fund-raising had been learned, however, the Society went from near-bankruptcy to prosperity very quickly.

Informals moved to the Apollo at Bulwell for a while and in October 1970 all meetings were transferred to the Carlton Forum and the C-3 was stored there, making things a bit easier.

November 1970 saw the first non-Hammond organ (a Baldwin) at a Recital (there had been one at an Informal previously). For many years, such events were extremely rare, but a Recital on the then latest Yamaha by Len Rawle in

November 1977 perhaps marked a turning point. From then on, other makes began to make regular appearances: one or two a year, then three or four, until by the mid 80s, roughly 50% of Recitals were on other makes. These were initially the classic American makes (Gulbransen, Lowrey etcetera), later overtaken by European instruments (Eminent, Hohner, Wersi). Demonstrations of various makes became a feature of Informals. The first criticism of the C-3 was raised at the 1983 AGM but was not widely accepted.

Back to the story: the end of our fifth year, 1972, was as significant as 1969 had been. In October, a brand new C-3 was purchased and proved a distinct improvement on the old one. Such was our financial position that the new organ was fully paid for within a year. At the AGM in November we voted (the Committee having discussed the matter with Hammonds and received their blessing) to become the Nottingham Organ Society. Although Recitals continued to be 99% Hammond for some years yet, many members (about half of them according to a survey conducted shortly afterwards) now owned different makes. It was in fairness to them, as well as establishing our independence that the name change was made. Also at the AGM we voted to buy a second smaller organ, though that did not materialise for some years.

A regime of power cuts in the early 1970s caused much shuffling of venues but we settled on Carlton Forum again for Recitals in October 1974, Informals being back at the Grey Goose. That year saw membership peak at 300, it began to fall off a little later but has been stable for many years since, in the upper 200s.

The January and February 1975 editions of *Harmony* introduced 'The Digital Revolution' and at the February Informal we had something of a coup when Carlo Curley demonstrated one of the then new Allen organs at the Grey Goose. The place was packed! In March 1976 we had our first band/variety show Informal – a memorable occasion – and in March 1977 our C-3 sported a pedal sustain system. At this time, many recitalists were bringing along string ensembles, synthesisers etcetera to sit on top of the C-3.

The 1970s had seen many special events, held at Stanford Hall, the Albert Hall and elsewhere. These had grown out of a need to raise funds, mentioned a bove, and they succeeded beyond all imagination. We featured Reginald Dixon no less that seven times, his farewell appearance in October 1978 being outstanding. It followed a Carlo Curley recital, also at the Albert Hall, earlier in the same month! A recent event on similar lines was the highly successful Phil Kelsall recital at the Mansfield Civic Theatre in April 1993.

Informals, meanwhile, moved to the Cavendish in Carlton, then the Nell

Gwynn in Bestwood and the Test Match in West Bridgford. The latter being rather out on a limb, was not a great success and attendance plummeted. However, a significant event, there was a demonstration of the then new Yamaha MR, MC and Clavinova in September 1985.

September 1984 saw a very favourable move when Recitals went to the Bonington Theatre in Arnold, where they have been held with great success ever since. Another key Recital was that by Paul Holmes on a Yamaha MC-600 in January 1986. Wersi and Technics had been very popular in the 1980s, but this, and the introduction of the Yamaha HS series – demonstrated at our July 1988 Informal – set the seal on future presentations. As we entered the 1990s, Yamaha HSs began to appear very regularly. In October 1990 Tina Kemp played an instrument made up from 'dumb' keyboards and MIDI expanders: perhaps the ultimate in hi-tech, but, surprisingly in a way, an idea that very few have taken up. Also in 1990 Informals went back to the Nell Gwynn for a while, but in June 1991 saw them return to the refurbished Cavendish where we have been very happy ever since. Our famous 'hands-on' Informals began their popular run at this time.

After 17 years of humping, bumping and misadventure, our C-3 had become very battered. It was disposed of in December 1989 and replaced by a good second-hand A-100. Recitals on hi-tech instruments brought along by the players were still running at about 50% of the total. The purchase of yet another Hammond was, in the words of Jim Turner in *Harmony,* to provide a contrast 'for those who like organ music' and 'what better than a Hammond tone-wheel?' There were still many who agreed with that, but a deep split was beginning to appear in the Society. In April 1991, a famous letter to *Harmony* suggesting that the A-100 was fit only for the dustbin (or wheelie-bin) immortalised the name of member Fred Clarey-Siddle.

In *Harmony* trade advertising had continued down the years, but by 1992 only one advertiser remained and the last advert appeared in February 1993. They had proved their worth at one time, but were an awful lot of trouble in more ways than one. Since we didn't really need the money any more they were happily dropped.

At the June 1993 Informal, the Society's Elka Portable made its debut, some twenty and a half years after it had been agreed to purchase a second organ! Like the Hammond, it found favour with some (largely the traditionalists) but not others. It did not remain our second organ for long, for in April 1995 an extraordinary general meeting was called to vote on the disposal of the A-100.

This was carried by a large majority, though the outcome was somewhat inevitable as the Committee had already disowned it for the reasons indicated above. Its final appearance was at a memorable Recital by Ken Stroud in September 1995. Within the month it was gone. Now it was all EL90s with big band and orchestral sounds. That's what the majority want and its by giving the people what they want that the Nottingham Organ Society has progressed (with its ups and downs like any other organisation) over 30 years into the successful society that it is today. We could do with a slightly better turnout, especially at Informals, but we have a great atmosphere and do very nicely. We have the top names at our Recitals and run some attractive special events and trips to places of interest. Some very talented members play at our Informals and our Christmas Parties are the highlights of the year. We go on confidently to the next 30 years.

Chapter 27

Nottingham Organ Society – The second 30 years 1997 to 2027?

By Michael Carpenter

The period around the turn of the millennium saw a plateau in the Nottingham Organ Society's fortunes.

We presented the Blackpool Tower Ballroom organist, Phil Kelsall, at the Mansfield Civic Centre in 1993, and then at the Palace Theatre, Newark, from 1998 to 2001. This raised a large amount of money for the Society, which would prove to be extremely valuable to us in later years.

Our co-founder, Mike Slater, now resident in Blackpool, became our President in 1999, and our membership peaked at 300 for a second time in 2000/1.

The millennium year 2000 was celebrated in style. All membership was free for the year; Stephen Foulkes appeared in a sell-out 'Last Night of the Proms' evening in January; a Society member, Councillor Dennis Walker, became Mayor of Gedling Borough and invited our President, Committee members and helpers to a superb reception at the Civic Centre in August; we took a coach trip to Blackpool to see Nigel Ogden and Kevin Grunill play the newly refurbished Opera House Wurlitzer in November; and in December *Harmony* got a new cover design.

Sadly, the period also saw the passing of a number of our old, stalwart members, including our other co-founder, Phylis Smedley in 1999, our first President, Denis Mathews MBE in 2004, and several notable former Committee members. Mike Slater died in 2008.

We also saw the beginning of a decline in attendances, notably at informals, and in membership from about 2005, which was the year in which we had our last recital sell-out, for Robert Wolfe. Advancing the start time for Recitals from 8 p.m to 6.30 p.m. did bring about a slight recovery in attendance, but the overriding trend from here on was a slow decline. In fact, it was not just our Society that was struggling: the instrument dealers in Nottingham and the surrounding district started closing down one by one, as did very many other organ societies around the country.

By the time we celebrated our 50th Anniversary in 2017, our membership was down to 155, only about half of its peak, and attendance at Recitals was only about half of the capacity of the Bonington Theatre. Then, of course, the Covid pandemic struck and our activities were suspended from March 2020 to July the following year. Most retail hospitality and leisure businesses, large and small, were also adversely impacted, many of them terminally, so we were perhaps lucky to have survived at all.

However, we could no longer support coach trips, Christmas parties or even Informal evenings and were able only to present Recitals (now called 'Performances') with attendances amounting now to barely a quarter of the Theatre's capacity, and we are losing money at every one. It is here that those funds created at Newark 20 years earlier came into their own to keep us going, but the trouble is, of course, that they can only last so long. We are trying our best to keep going for as long as we can, but, it pains me to say the whole organ scene is in terminal decline. Young people no longer have an interest in 'traditional' music or in solo instrumental performances, and we are stuck with an ageing membership. How much longer we can last is unknown, but it seems unlikely that we will make our 60th year in 2027.

One initiative we have been trying with some success is to put on some 'Variety' shows, with solo and ensemble singers, other instrumentalists and groups, comedy, magic and such, to try to appeal to a wider, non-specific audience, and particularly to younger people. These have been created and master-minded by our Committee member Mark Everatt, but they take such a tremendous time and effort to organise that they cannot be presented as often as we would like. They could perhaps offer just a small glimmer of hope.

All things considered, we have had a long run and have done well – better, indeed, than many or most other organ societies, so whatever befalls us we have much to be proud of.

Chapter 28

St Peter's Ravenshead Gilbert & Sullivan Society

I have been attending operas performed by the St Peter's Ravenshead Gilbert & Sullivan Society for over 30 years. The village of Ravenshead is situated on the A60 Road, close to Newstead Abbey Gates and between Arnold and Mansfield. Performances take place in the Village Hall and are accompanied by piano. They suffered the loss of many members during the Covid outbreak in 2020 and restarted their activities with concert performances of The Mikado in St Peter's Church, Sheepwalk Lane in February 2023. I was invited to video the production and was delighted to accept but requested to be situated on the front row. They agreed so I obtained good sound and vision quality. I edited the performance into 5 parts and loaded them to YouTube with these titles

Mikado, Concert Version, Part 1 St Peter's Church, Ravenshead G&S Nottingham

Date viewed:

Mikado Concert Version, Part 2 St Peter's Church, Ravenshead G&S, Nottingham

Date viewed:

Mikado Concert Version, Part 3 St Peter's Church, Ravenshead G&S Nottingham

Date viewed:

Mikado Concert Version, Part 4 St Peter's Church, Ravenshead G&S, Nottingham

Date viewed:

Mikado Concert Version, Part 5 St Peter's Church, Ravenshead G&S, Nottingham

Date viewed:

The Society performed a varied selection of songs at St Peter's Church, on Sheepwalk Lane, during June 2023. Here are six YouTube titles that I invite you to watch.

June, words by Nora Hopper, music by Roger Quilter Sung by Helen

Date viewed:

When Britain Really Ruled the Waves, G & S, Iolanthe Ravenshead, Nottingham

Date viewed:

When a Merry Maiden Marries, Gilbert and Sullivan, The Gondoliers, Ravenshead June 2023

Date viewed:

Don't put your daughter on the stage Mrs Worthington, Shakespearean performance

Date viewed:

You Raise Me Up, St Peters Church, Ravenshead, Nottingham, 3 June 23

Date viewed:

Jerusalem sung by Ravenshead G & S, Nottinghamshire, June 2023

Date viewed:

They returned to the Village Hall to perform a fully costumed version of HMS Pinafore in February 2024. I loaded the complete performance to YouTube in two parts. You can view them by using these titles

HMS Pinafore, Act 1, Gilbert & Sullivan, St Peter's Ravenshead Nottingham, MD Stephen Godward

Date viewed:

HMS Pinafore, Act 2 Gilbert & Sullivan, St Peter's Ravenshead Nottingham, MD Stephen Godward

Date viewed:

On 18 May 2024 the Society performed a concert which they called 'Showstoppers' in St Peter's Church at Ravenshead. On the following day they came to the Arnold Community Centre and repeated the show. I videoed this event and have loaded some of the songs to YouTube with these titles

t's a Grand Night for Singing, State Fair, in concert at Arnold Community Centre May 2024

Date viewed:

Edelweiss from The Sound of Music. Arnold Community Centre near Nottm May 2024

Date viewed:

It's Harry I'm planning to Marry, Calamity Jane performed by Georgie Lee

Date viewed:

Anthem from Chess sung by Andy Rushton at Arnold Nottm 19 May 2024

Date viewed:

Wouldn't it be Loverly & Just you wait Henry Higgins, My Fair Lady, Cynthia Marriott & Jane Stubbs

Date viewed:

The Girl in 14G from Let yourself Go, Sung by Joanne Kay, May 2024

Date viewed:

I Remember it Well, Gigi, Karen Turner & Chris Kenny at Arnold Community Centre 2024

Date viewed:

When the Foeman, From The Pirates of Penzance, Ravenshead G & S Society

Date viewed:

This is the Moment, Jekyll & Hyde, Arnold/Nottm Summer Concert 2024

Date viewed:

The next planned event is Gilbert & Sullivan's The Sorcerer to be performed at Ravenshead Village Hall from 19 to 22 February 2025.

Chapter 29
St Peter's Ravenshead Gilbert & Sullivan Society
Written by Karen Turner with help from Alan Browne and Ron Walker

Mary Williamson lived most of her life in Ravenshead. In 1936 she moved into a newly built detached house on Longdale Lane in Ravenshead. She was a teacher of French at Queen Elizabeth School in Mansfield for many years and said that during the second world war both male and female staff had to be addressed as "Sir". Equality for women is nothing new! A lifelong member of St. Peter's Church, she sang in the Choir until her health started to fail. When she died in 1999, aged 85, she was buried wearing a Choir robe and interred with her mother in Blidworth Parish Church.

In 1952 she started a small group of St Peter's Church members singing G & S numbers – she was passionate about G & S. Mary was the founder of St Peter's Ravenshead Gilbert & Sullivan Society back in 1954, before the present Church was even built. The first staged opera was in 1957 with Mikado, always a favourite even now with our audiences. The Church was originally the building which became the hall and was erected in 1948. When the very modern building was built in 1972, a bell-housing was on the roof with a French Monastery bell ringing out each Sunday. This bell was donated by Mary after she went to a redundant Church in France to bring it back to Ravenshead. Although no longer used, the bell is still in the Sacristy of the Church.

The Society developed from Mary's passion for music and was made up primarily of Choir members. They performed on a small stage at the back of the Church hall. When I moved into the village in 1993, the curtains still hung there though I never saw them closed as G & S was long gone to its new home and the stage had disappeared. Mary virtually ran everything with St. Peter's congregation taking part and doing all the front and back stage roles. The success of the Society's reputation travelled further afield and others joined from out of the area.

Mary had an excellent tenor voice and took many lead parts as well as Producer, Musical Director and rehearsal pianist. She played piano for many years for the nights of the show and often towards the end of the week her fingers were bandaged due to soreness. Nothing would stop her making her contribution.

Ron and Pat Walker came into the village in 1970 and Pat, soon after, joined the Society. A new Director was needed and Pat decided that Ron could stand in for a year as he had done some producing before. Ron soon found himself with a job that no-one else wanted for many years. A little like today. I was going to do the role of the Secretary for a couple of years, but one thing after another stopped me from handing over the mantle and I have been doing it for five years and counting. It was her commitment and enthusiasm for G & S which was infectious and indeed was the reason why, when she approached Alan Browne in 1988 to help with set building for Iolanthe, he could not resist! This led to him being on stage in the chorus the next year for "Pirates of Penzance" (the last one Ron Walker produced). There was then a gap and it was Mary who suggested, encouraged and bullied him into becoming the producer for the next two productions – "The Mikado "and "Princess Ida". She was the sort of person no-one could not say no to, mainly out of admiration but also a touch of fear! When Mary sadly died in 1999 the Church was full to overflowing at her funeral, such was the esteem in which she was held. The Church Choir sang "Drop, drop slow tears" by Orlando Gibbons and also "Rejoice in the Lord Always" by Henry Purcell, also known as "The Bell Anthem".

In 1968 the cornerstone of the Village Hall was laid by Princess Alice, Countess of Athlone after many years of fundraising. Eventually, the Church Hall was no longer big enough for the loyal audiences and the stage proved to be too small to accommodate the chorus and principals. The Society moved to Ravenshead Village Hall in the 70s to perform and remain there now. The

Society instigated the opening up of the room under the stage in the Hall. Prior to this, if anyone needed to go onto the stage from a different side to the one they came off, they would have to go outside, using the doors in the Brammar Room and the car park. As the Society performed then and still do now in February half term, it was often snowing, and the ladies, often wearing ballet shoes, would be drenched, ruining wigs, shoes, costumes and make-up as they entered stage left after exiting stage right.

All of the shows have been performed over the years, including The Zoo (not strictly G & S), The Duke (which was adapted by Ron as the Frightfully Grand Duke concert style) and Trial by Jury (completely sung). I don't really have a favourite, but enjoy lots of them for lots of different reasons. Pirates was the first I sang, Pinafore was the first I watched. Mikado was the first I performed with Ravenshead. Iolanthe had the women as fairies with dresses which lit up with fairy lights in the second act. Very dramatic. I loved the costumes for Sorcerer where I dressed as the downstairs maid. I always had to go 'round the back', being rudely refused entry with the other servants by the Butler, played by Trevor Tagg. At the very end everyone went off with the person they had fallen in love with. I was left alone until the butler came back on, beckoned me over and kissed me on the cheek. My leg came up at the back, rather like a black and white movie heroine and the audience 'aah' -ed every time. I enjoyed Princess Ida for the strong female role. Utopia was set for us on another planet and saw me dressed in silver boots, a silver dress and a purple tinsel wig. I loved the make up which was also purple and glittery. I enjoy being in the chorus. I find I can over-act to my heart's content and no-one is really paying me much attention. I am not brave enough to sing alone or have people watch me speak.

The pandemic saw us rehearsing Mikado. We had already rehearsed the music and knew that off book. We were setting the performance and learning dances, when to get on, who we should be standing next to at what part and how to huddle. Our current Producer is fond of a huddle which is used for dramatic tension and eye contact with the audience. The news came through and we were devastated. Not only would we not be able to put on the show but all the costs so far of rehearsing would not be recouped. Since 1957, there have been years when no production was put on. Originally, the Society performed every two years. Sometimes a concert was put on instead of a full show but since 1982 there has been a show every year. We missed singing and our singing friends and were lost on Tuesday evenings which is our rehearsal night.

We began again, after the first lockdown finished, thinking that we could now get back to normal. It was a joy to see everyone again, even though we rehearsed within the conditions laid out for us in terms of social distancing, mask wearing, hand sanitising and opening windows. Like the rest of the country we couldn't believe it when it happened again. This time was not as strict with different rules being laid out. There were possibilities for us to sing. We could do it outside. We were allowed an audience as long as they were metres apart. We could do a concert instead. We could stand on stage, although I cannot remember how we would have got around the distancing and how far apart we had to be. The committee decided to vote. The whole Society was given a choice and a slip of paper. By one vote, it was decided we would not be singing for another year. Counting the votes was agony for several of us. We were so desperate to be singing again and doing something normal. In hindsight, it was the right decision even if I didn't agree at the time. Logic and common sense won out. So we performed Yeoman of the Guard in 2020 and staged a comeback in 2023 in the old venue, St Peter's (although in the Church rather than the hall, which was then rebuilt as the Centre) by creating Mikado, the staged version. All the songs were there, but a lot of the dialogue was cut. Instead there was a narrator (me) and the cast were static apart from the principals. The production went down well but the audience wanted us back in the hall and they wanted comfortable seats rather than hard wooden pews.

A year after I joined the Society, in 2012, we needed a new Director. Our Musical Director Linda Harvey knew of someone who had had success in other Societies, had a good reputation and had an unusual theme for Utopia Ltd. As a Society we have to vote for the people who direct us and it was a landslide vote that enabled us to work with Stephen Godward. Previously a music teacher, he directs other choirs and sings Gilbert and Sullivan professionally, as well as singing in pantomimes and on cruises. His aim was to produce all of the operas with us and once the Gondoliers has been done he will have achieved this goal. We are hoping he continues after that! Stephen continues to have original ideas for us and enables us to have the wonderful sound we create by his extraordinary musical talent and patience. A quote from the reviewer on Kev Castle's Theatre Review, said, "St Peter's G & S Society are a brilliant company who specialise in the works of Gilbert and Sullivan, and that love of these two shone through their work. Their comedy is sharp and their singing is powerful and expressive, drawing all the individual emotions from every piece they perform."

February 2024 saw us going back to the stage in the Village Hall, which we love. Each year we strive to have something which attracts and intrigues our audiences. HMS Pinafore had us all on the stage for the whole of Act 1, with a set consisting of flags and fairy lights. It was very dramatic. Ludwig, a baby grand piano was introduced which enhanced the sound of the accompaniment. February 2025 will be The Sorcerer and will include children from the local dance school as sprites dancing, as villagers and as a page.

We are so blessed to have many talented and generous members and it truly feels like home and family to belong to the Society. It's part of the history of our village and I have worked really hard to ensure it keeps going for many more years. Even if you have never watched a G & S production, give it a go. The stories are ludicrous but the settings are fabulous and the singing is amazing.

Here is a list of the productions that the Society has performed since we started in 1957.

1957	The Mikado
1959	The Gondoliers
1960	Patience
1962	Ruddigore
1964	Iolanthe
1965	Yeomen of the Guard
1966	Princess Ida
1968	Utopia Limited
1969	The Mikado
1970	The Sorcerer
1971	The Gondoliers
1972	Ruddigore
1973	HMS Pinafore
1974	Princess Ida
1974	Trial by Jury (July Concert)
1975	Pirates of Penzance
1976	Patience
1977	Iolanthe
1978	The Mikado
1979	Princess Ida
1980	Utopia Limited
1982	HMS Pinafore
1983	Patience
1984	Yeomen of the Guard

1985	Ruddigore
1986	The Gondoliers
1987	The Sorcerer
1988	Iolanthe
1989	Pirates of Penzance
1990	The Mikado
1991	Princess Ida
1992	HMS Pinafore & Trial by Jury
1993	Patience
1994	Ruddigore
1995	Yeomen of the Guard
1996	The Gondoliers
1997	The Sorcerer
1997	The Zoo & Trial by Jury (July Concert)
1998	Pirates of Penzance
1998	Frightfully Grand Duke (Concert)
1999	Iolanthe
2000	Utopia Limited
2001	The Mikado
2002	Princess Ida
2003	HMS Pinafore
2004	Yeomen of the Guard
2005	Ruddigore
2006	The Gondoliers
2007	Patience
2008	Pirates of Penzance
2009	The Sorcerer
2010	Iolanthe
2011	The Mikado
2012	Utopia Limited
2013	HMS Pinafore & Trial by Jury
2014	Princess Ida
2015	Ruddigore
2016	The Sorcerer
2017	Patience
2018	Pirates of Penzance
2019	Iolanthe

2020   Yeomen of the Guard
2023   The Mikado
2024   HMS Pinafore

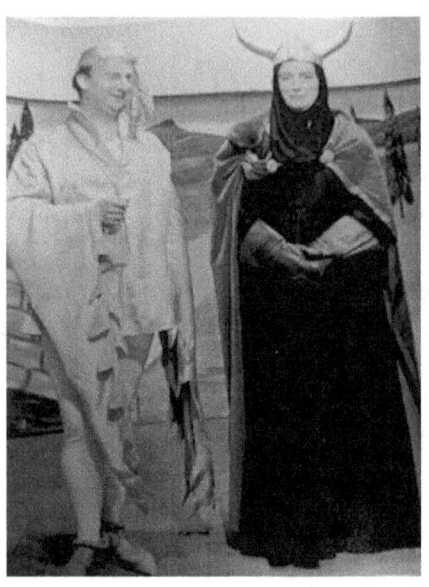

Mary Williamson on stage with Charles Bramley. Mary is revered as the founder of the St Peter's Ravenshead Gilbert and Sullivan Society.

CHAPTER 30
ERIC COATES SOCIETY

I joined the Eric Coates Society in 2011 and have videoed at some of the concerts they promoted at the Central Methodist Church in Hucknall, Nottinghamshire. The venue is less than a mile from where Eric was born on 27 August 1886. His father was the local doctor and his mother an excellent pianist, an attribute that proved useful to Eric as he took an interest in music. The family lived in a large house on Tenter Hill, Hucknall (this was renamed Byron Street some years later). He had three sisters and one brother and appeared to have a happy childhood. He pestered his parents to get him a violin after hearing one being played and a very small brightly coloured red and yellow one was given to him when he was six years old. The Coates children did not go to school but were educated at home by a governess who Eric did not like because he wanted to be studying music, everything else was unimportant to him. Not content with playing violin, he also started to learn to play piano with help from his Mother. When Eric was a boy transport was by train, coach and horses or pony and trap. The motor car had not become available at that time. As Eric grew older he progressed to playing a viola which he bought from a music shop in Goldsmith Street, Nottingham. He also joined an orchestra which played four concerts a year in Nottingham's Albert Hall and he became determined to take up music as a profession. His Father was not keen on the idea because he knew what a precarious life musicians led, instead, he encouraged his son to take a job in a bank. Eric hated the idea so the debate lingered on until a friend, who had been to the Royal Academy of Music, had tea with the family. The friend said to Eric's Father 'Doctor, you must let Eric go to the Academy and get him with Lionel Tertis for viola and Frederick Corder for Composition'. Father relented and arranged for Eric to go to the Academy for a year but said, 'If it doesn't work out you must take up the bank job'.

The Royal Academy of Music was on Tenterden Street, Hanover Square in those days. Eric was nineteen when he arrived in the early Autumn of 1906. Before being accepted as a student he had to pass an audition with the Principal Sir Alexander Campbell Mackenzie who, as the name suggests, was Scottish. This consisted of presenting examples of his composition work and playing a piece on viola. The Principal gave Eric the news that he had passed the tests and was to be admitted as a student of the Academy with a rather strange comment. 'Mark my words young man, you will start as a viola player but you will end up as a composer'.

History has shown how true these words were but they did not come to fruition not until many years later. Eric worked diligently on his studies and started to earn money by accepting offers to play in various orchestras and theatres in the evenings. He had acquired a very large viola and started to experience constant pain in his left hand. This spread into his arm and despite some form of 'electrical' treatment became worse. He completed his first year at the Academy and stayed in London and became a viola player with the 'Queen's Hall Orchestra' which had the word 'Light' added to the title some years later.

On the 4th of March 1911 Eric attended a student concert at the Royal Academy of Music and an interesting situation developed. He and another former RAM student went to a Friday night concert and were given a programme on the way in. They noticed that one of the items was billed as a 'Recitation' and decided that they were in for a good laugh. They noted the name of the new student, Phyllis Black, and made up their minds that she was going to be ridiculously awful. Later, they watched in stunned silence as a charming little girl, who appeared to be about sixteen, walked on stage and recited Tennyson's 'Mermaid'. Eric was captivated by the girl and thought that the words would be charming if put to music so decided that he must meet her. At the end of the concert he looked around but saw no sight of his dream girl. He did see a friend who was a member of the Academy staff and asked him to provide details of the recitalist. His friend asked Eric to see him on the following Monday morning and said he would 'see what he could do'. On the following Monday Eric enlisted the help of his friend and managed to meet Phyllis on the pretext that he wanted to write music to accompany her poetry reading. They met in a small room and discussed the music idea at first before talking about their families and other subjects. It was getting towards closing time so Eric escorted Phyllis to a tea shop where they found a quiet position and continued their conversation, many subjects were discussed, one of the most important was their respective ages. Eric was twenty-five and Phyllis sixteen but one day before her seventeenth birthday which was the following day. It was 'love at first sight' when Eric had seen Phyllis on stage and reciprocated when Phyllis, whose family lived in North London, met Eric on that Monday. It was getting late so they went together into the street, holding hands as they walked to Regent Street, where the horse-bus was about to leave to take Phyllis home. Eric went to a flower shop and organised a bunch of red roses and wrote a card, to be sent to her home address.

Eric had a pre arranged visit to friends in Gloucestershire the following day and returned to London on the Friday. He went to the Academy to collect Phyllis from her lesson in the afternoon and received devastating news, her family did not approve of Eric but wanted to meet him the following day. He duly went to the home in North London but received a cold reception and his suggestion that they should be married immediately was definitely not even considered. When meeting Phyllis on the following Monday she said that her family had decided that she was not to meet him again because she was too young. They decided to see each other every day but tried to keep their meetings discreet. However, that did not stop Eric being tactfully warned about his relationship with Phyllis by senior management of the Academy. They then received an invitation to tea by some members of her family but her Father made an unexpected appearance. He marched them to the family house where they were lectured by both angry parents who stated that Eric could go to the family home on some Sundays but they were not allowed to see each other at any other time. The young couple took no notice of this instruction and continued to meet regularly. Early in 1912 they went to a shop on Regent Street where Eric bought a diamond ring and they pledged their engagement to be married.

Phyllis's father was a Frenchman and the family had arranged that she, against her wishes, would stay in a cottage near Calais for the Winter vacation in 1913. Eric was invited to go there in January and was immediately involved in a heated family discussion with Phyllis and her parents. Eventually Phyllis delivered an ultimatum, saying, 'You know, Mother, if you do not allow us to be married now, one day you will go up to my room to find my bed has not been slept in!' After a long pause came the words 'Very well children'. The couple were married on 3 February 1913 but Phyllis retained her surname, Black, to follow her ambition to be an actress.

Alick Maclean was the conductor of the Queens Hall Light Orchestra and during the short summer season went to Yorkshire where he conducted the Scarborough Orchestra. He asked Eric to go up there in the Summer of 1919 to conduct some of his own compositions that were often included in their concerts, he thoroughly enjoyed doing this for a few years. In July 1919 Eric received a letter terminating his role as viola player in the Queens Hall Orchestra and vowed never to play the viola again as he had to suffer intense pain from the neuritis in his left arm. His plan was to concentrate on composition work. A son, Austin, was born on 16 April 1922 just after the family moved to live in Hampstead Garden Suburb.

The Eric Coates Society presented a concert at the Central Methodist Church, Hucknall, Nottingham on 6 October 2012. It included Japanese pianist Haruko Seki who is an ardent admirer of the music of Eric Coates. Every summer she goes to her native country and promotes his music there.

The YouTube titles are

        Sleepy Lagoon, Eric Coates, Haruko Seki, piano

Date viewed:

        Bird Songs at Eventide, Eric Coates, Haruko Seki, piano

Date viewed:

        Joyous Youth from Three Elizabeths Suite, Eric Coates, Haruko Seki Piano

Date viewed:

        Knightsbridge March, Eric Coates, London Suite, Haruko Seki, piano

Date viewed:

        Tit for Tat, Eric Coates, words by William Lyle, Haruko Seki, piano

Date viewed:

My YouTube Adventures

Other titles from Michael Parkinson

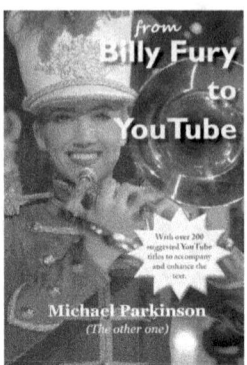

From Billy Fury to YouTube ISBN 978-1-78222-588-1

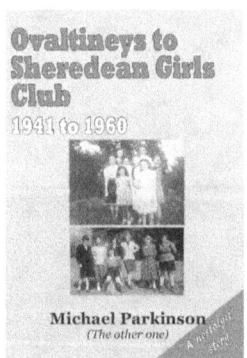

Ovaltineys to Sheredean Girls Club ISBN 978-1-78222-675-8

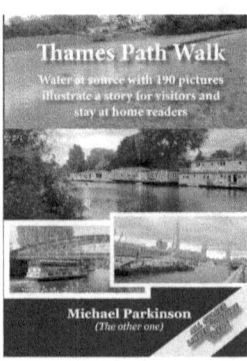

Thames Path Walk ISBN 978-1-78222-755-7

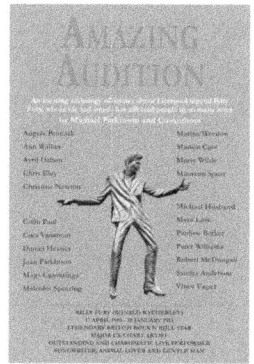

Amazing Audition ISBN 978-1-78222-831-8

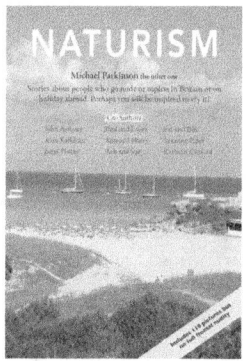

Naturism ISBN 978-1-78222-916-2